Nuclear and Toxic Waste

Other books in the At Issue series:

At ✳ Issue

Nuclear and Toxic Waste

Stuart A. Kallen, *Book Editor*

Bruce Glassman, *Vice President*
Bonnie Szumski, *Publisher*
Helen Cothran, *Managing Editor*

GREENHAVEN PRESS
An imprint of Thomson Gale, a part of The Thomson Corporation

THOMSON
✳
™
GALE

Detroit • New York • San Francisco • San Diego • New Haven, Conn.
Waterville, Maine • London • Munich

For more information, contact
Greenhaven Press
27500 Drake Rd.
Farmington Hills, MI 48331-3535
Or you can visit our Internet site at http://www.gale.com

LIBRARY OF CONGRESS CATALOGING-IN-PUBLICATION DATA
Nuclear and toxic waste / Stuart A. Kallen, book editor. p. cm. — (At issue) Includes bibliographical references and index. ISBN 0-7377-2190-1 (lib. : alk. paper) — ISBN 0-7377-2191-X (pbk. : alk. paper) 1. Hazardous waste—United States. 2. Hazardous waste sites—United States. 3. Radioactive waste disposal—United States. I. Kallen, Stuart A., 1955– . II. At issue (San Diego, Calif.) TD1040.N83 2005 363.72'87—dc22   2004060691

Printed in the United States of America

Contents

Introduction

In the past century, the United States has been transformed from a largely agricultural society to an industrial and military superpower. During this metamorphosis, the environment has been radically altered by motor vehicles, chemical factories, hazardous waste sites, nuclear power plants, and military weapons facilities. These sources produce toxic waste that includes dioxins, polychlorinated biphenyls (PCBs), heavy metals, nerve gas, uranium fuel rods, and plutonium bomb parts. This pollution contaminates the land, air, water, and even the human body.

The statistics concerning toxic substances are mind-boggling. Since World War II, industry has introduced more than seventy thousand chemicals now regularly in use. They include a wide variety of dangerous chemicals, such as arsenic, chlorine, cyanide, creosote, mercury, benzene, chromium, and toluene. Thousands have nearly unpronounceable names, such as dichloromethylphenylsilane. These substances are used by industry to manufacture products such as plastics, herbicides, building materials, batteries, and a host of industrial solvents, cleaners, and lubricants. They are produced in some of the twelve thousand chemical manufacturing plants in the United States and warehoused in more than four hundred thousand major storage facilities.

People throughout the world have come to depend on the products of the chemical industry, and there is scarcely a household anywhere on the planet that does not contain at least a few items made from toxic substances. However, environmentalists say that these goods come at a price. The chemical industry is the number one producer of toxic pollution, and, again, the numbers are staggering. According to the Toxic Release Inventory (TRI), a list of 650 industrial chemicals tracked by the Environmental Protection Agency (EPA), about twenty-five thousand facilities create nearly a billion pounds of hazardous waste annually. About half of this waste is released into the air, about 200 million pounds are pumped into the earth in underground injection wells, and 90 million pounds are dumped into rivers, lakes, and oceans. Nearly 45 million pounds are disposed of at hazardous waste dumps. The rest is burned or recycled for other industrial uses, such as cement and asphalt production.

Like nearly every other matter involving environmental problems, public health, government oversight, and corporate responsibility, the TRI is controversial. Environmentalists point out that at least 330 million pounds of various toxins are omitted from the list. Conversely, some business interests claim that the information in the TRI is manipulated by people with political agendas. As Dale E. Klein, vice chancellor for Special Engineering Programs at the University of Texas, states:

> TRI's definition of a chemical "release" is too broad, has nothing to do with health effects, and its raw numbers are used by professional and semi-professional environmental activists to scare people who live near industrial plants. . . . Yet some self-appointed guardians of the environment regard the inventory as the nation's annual environmental report card.

Another controversial element of the toxic waste management debate is a law known as the Comprehensive Environmental Response, Compensation, and Liability Act or simply the "Superfund." Created in 1980 to clean up hazardous waste sites, chemical spills, accidents, and emergency releases of toxins into the environment, the Superfund is criticized by both environmentalists and corporate interests. Although 70 million people, including 10 million children, live within four miles of one of the nation's 1,230 Superfund sites, cleanup has been dogged by lawsuits and other troubles, while very few of the designated sites have ever been made safe.

The Superfund is paid for by a special tax on all chemical and petrochemical producers. All manufacturers are taxed whether or not they actually create toxic waste sites. This form of taxation has been widely criticized by business interests who believe that individual polluters, rather than all chemical manufacturers, should pay for site cleanup. As Angela Logomasini writes in *National Review Online*, "the Superfund principle could be called the 'everyone is guilty principle.'" Environmentalists also find fault with the Superfund law and the EPA's role in fulfilling its requirements. They point out that even though more contaminated sites are discovered every year, the EPA continues to make drastic cuts in its budget for toxic waste cleanup.

While the EPA struggles with pollution produced by private

businesses, it also has a mandate to regulate pollution created by the government and the military. This task is challenging because the federal government is responsible for creating tons of toxic and nuclear waste. According to environmentalist Bob Feldmen in *Dollars and Sense:*

> The U.S. Department of Defense is . . . the world's largest polluter, producing more hazardous waste per year than the five largest U.S. chemical companies combined. . . . Just about every U.S. military base and nuclear arms facility emits toxics into the environment. At many U.S. military target ranges, petroleum products and heavy metals used in bombs and bullets contaminate the soil and groundwater. . . . The contaminants . . . from military bases [also] include pesticides, solvents, petroleum, lead, mercury, and uranium. The health effects for the surrounding communities are devastating: miscarriages, low birth weights, birth defects, kidney disease, and cancer.

Despite complaints by environmentalists, the military wants to be exempt from laws regulating toxic and nuclear waste. Deputy Undersecretary of Defense Paul Mayberry speaks for many military leaders when he states that laws governing hazardous waste are putting the nation's military readiness at stake by restricting areas where bombs, bullets, and military chemicals can be used in training: "When you try to apply absolute, inflexible rules, what we have are no longer training ranges and installations but wildlife refuges and wilderness areas. . . . We have to ensure we can maintain the military uses of our installations and how they were originally designated for training requirements." Environmentalists argue, however, that military readiness has never been compromised because of restrictions in environmentally sensitive areas.

Another problem that pits some government officials against environmentalists and community activists concerns waste disposal at more than one hundred nuclear power plants throughout the country. Currently, worn-out uranium rods that have been used to produce electricity are stored outdoors in pools near nuclear reactors. Experts agree that the nuclear fuel is vulnerable to terrorists who could use it to produce devastating "dirty bombs." However, the experts disagree on what to do with this high-level radioactive waste, which will remain toxic for an estimated 240,000 years. Government officials want to transport the rods to a permanent repository built under Yucca Mountain in Nevada. Supporters of this plan believe that permanent, deep underground storage is the only safe way to dispose of this waste. Activists argue that shipping waste to Yucca Mountain will increase the terrorist threat by putting nuclear waste on the country's rails and roads. Although President George W. Bush ended a twenty-year political fight by designating Yucca Mountain as the nation's official radioactive waste disposal site in July 2002, the state of Nevada immediately sued the federal government, and the issue has yet to be decided by the courts.

Clearly, people disagree greatly about how to solve the problem of nuclear and toxic waste. As industry and government continue to produce billions of tons of toxins every year, it is certain that the debates will continue for many years to come.

1

Chemical Weapons Incineration Threatens Surrounding Communities

Matt Jones

Matt Jones is a member of Earth First!, a grassroots organization that fights environmental destruction using the legal process, civil disobedience, and sabotage of industrial equipment and structures.

In August 2003, the Department of Defense began the long process of destroying hundreds of old, obsolete chemical weapons in high-tech incinerators in Anniston, Alabama. Military officials claim that these weapons must be demolished before they accidentally detonate and kill hundreds of people. However, those who live in Anniston are bearing the brunt of this government decision. The incinerator emits cancer-causing air pollution when the weapons are burned. Furthermore, an accident might occur when the weapons are being moved to the incinerator. This would send toxic plumes of deadly gas into nearby homes, schools, and businesses. In the event of such an emergency, the army expects the men, women, children, and senior citizens in the community to protect themselves by quickly securing sheets of plastic over their windows and doors with duct tape. While government officials insist that there is little chance that such an event can occur, uncertainty grips the community. There are better ways to dispose of chemical weapons, and the military should stop this dangerous incineration before tragedy results.

The threat of weapons of mass destruction comes not from Iraq, but from here in the US. Ask anyone living near the eight US chemical weapons (CW) stockpiles in Colorado, Oregon, Utah, Arkansas, Alabama, Indiana, Maryland, and Kentucky to point them out.

> *More than 80 known waste products are released into the air we breathe by CW [chemical weapons] incineration, including dioxins, heavy metals and PCBs.*

As a result of CW incineration, southern Appalachia is being poisoned by chronic toxic emissions. These emissions do not stop at the state line; I live downwind from the Anniston Army Depot (ANAD) in Anniston, Alabama, as does most of my family here in Georgia. More than 80 known waste products are released into the air we breathe by CW incineration, including dioxins, heavy metals and PCBs. These emissions, through bioaccumulation [slowly accumulating in the body] or simple exposure, can lead to cancer and immune system damage, as well as reproductive and developmental problems in humans and wildlife.

In 1963, ANAD began storing VX nerve gas and GB sarin and mustard gas munitions in concrete and earthen igloos without informing the locals. It was not until 1988, when the Army broke ground on its Anniston incinerator, that many residents discovered that they lived next to a time bomb. Munitions began leaking because of faulty manufacturing, causing toxic clouds. In 1997, the US ratified the Chemical Weapons Convention, setting a 2007 deadline for the destruction of all CW stockpiles with an optional five year extension. Out of the eight remaining stockpiles in the US, four are slated for incineration; others will be destroyed using a safer neutralization process.

Anniston residents are claiming environmental discrimination, considering that 44 percent of the population is African American. More than 24 percent of the city's population is living below the poverty line. Thirty-five thousand residents live within nine miles of the incinerator.

Anniston officials have called it a patriotic duty to burn CW, and it became a state's rights issue with the state losing. The Federal Emergency Management Agency [FEMA] didn't support the incineration plan, deeming evacuation out of Anniston impossible. In the end, compromises between politicians, the Alabama Department of Environmental Mismanagement (ADEM) and the Army bought "Maximum Protection" with sheet plastic, duct tape, scissors, and cheap plastic gas mask "Scape hoods" and CW education by Centech, a private contractor distributing hoods and information to Anniston residents. A six-county-wide drill was conducted on March 10 [2004], including all of the surrounding Alabama counties' Emergency Management Agencies (EMA) and first responders. No citizens were involved.

"Chop and Drop"

ANAD has a permit for a dangerous practice called "chop and drop." CW incinerators were designed to burn liquid forms of mustard, sarin and VX agents. Problems arose when it was discovered that many munitions agents had gelled or crystallized due to age or faulty manufacturing. Liquid agent is drained and burned separately from the munitions casings, but with gelled agent, the rocket is just chopped and burned. This can lead to incomplete destruction of the live agent, because liquid agent vaporizes much faster when exposed to flame than a large piece of metal exposed to the same flame.

> *The Army is stubbornly refusing to change its monitors and continues to burn these hellish Cold War weapons.*

The Tooele, Utah, incinerator is allowed to chop and drop one munition per hour. ADEM, however, granted the ANAD permission to chop and drop between nine and 34 rockets per hour. Production or destruction is the only objective in the minds of the Anniston incinerator crews, leaving area residents as unwilling guinea pigs during this "ramping up" to the top speed of 34 rockets per hour.

ADEM and the Environmental "Protection" Agency (EPA) set up smokestack monitors after a 760-hour, unmonitored trial burn for each chemical agent, even though many potentially unknown agents—such as EA 2192, which is formed when VX and water vapor mix—are un-monitorable by this method. For one to two weeks, the agencies monitor emissions levels based on furnace temperature and the duration of the burn. Meeting ADEM and EPA air quality standards allows the ANAD to burn indefinitely and without oversight until they start burning a different CW. Passing or not passing these tests obviously has no effect on whether the incinerator still burns. Recently in Anniston, the incinerator failed its PCB trial but was allowed to continue burning above EPA levels until it was able to pass a second trial.

Outdated Technology

Furthermore, the Army is using outdated 1982 technology to monitor for mustard, sarin and VX nerve gases only. As agent is burned, the pollution plume drifts over a monitor and is collected in air tubes. If an alarm sounds, a worker analyzes the tubes in a laboratory, testing only for live agent. This process takes at least 20 minutes.

> *Do we have to wait until people die from exposure to CW or [the emissions]?*

Congress and the National Research Council continue to suggest that the Army needs to update its monitors to new infrared spectroscopy that can detect multiple toxins, including EA 2192, simultaneously over a large area. The response time for these monitors is approximately 10 seconds. But the Army is stubbornly refusing to change its monitors and continues to burn these hellish Cold War weapons. In addition, it is using 1972 chemical exposure levels set for healthy male soldiers to decide if a live agent release is high enough to warrant sounding an alarm. These levels are far above the EPA's Federal Register of Acute Exposure Guidelines and were criticized as too high by a 1994 Department of Defense report.

On February 4 [2004], two workers were exposed to GB sarin

gas inside an observation deck of the incinerator, causing an evacuation of the complex. No gas was supposed to be in that part of the plant, and representatives said it might have come through the air filtration system—exposing another persistent, unresolved problem. The Anniston EMA was not notified until three hours later. This is not an isolated event.

Georgia's population and government officials are turning a blind eye to the incinerator directly upwind. Floyd and Carroll counties are only 40 miles east of ANAD; neither county was included in the March emergency drill. Floyd County's EMA has no plans for dealing with agent release and the hysteria that will ensue. People in Georgia say that it is the problem of those Alabama folks.

Opposing Disposal

Many groups have sprung up in response to the Army's abuse of the environment and local residents. The Chemical Weapons Working Group (CWWG), based in Berea, Kentucky, has been a leader in opposing the Army's flawed CW disposal plans. CWWG totes that "no emissions are good emissions," favoring neutralization over incineration because it doesn't risk releasing unmonitored toxic emissions.

I propose opening a new front of attack against the as-of-yet-un-touched Washington Group International, which is based in Boise, Idaho. The Earth-hating corporation owns and operates three of the four incinerators in the US and one neutralization plant in Colorado. Its website boasts a good working relationship with the Occupational Safety and Health Administration in the areas of ergonomics, hearing and crane safety while totally ignoring the danger to their workforce inside malfunctioning incinerators. Its environmental destruction days must be stopped. . . . Do we have to wait until people die from exposure to CW or [the emissions]? . . .

As a resident of southern Appalachia, I realize that these toxic chemicals need to be destroyed, but I also demand recognition and use of safer alternatives similar to the ones being used at other CW stockpiles in this country. Give us clean air, not chronic toxic emissions.

2

The Military Safely Incinerates Chemical Weapons

U.S. Army Chemical Materials Agency

The purpose of the U.S. Army Chemical Materials Agency is to protect and safely store the nation's aging chemical weapons while working toward the effective treatment and elimination of the nation's unused chemical warfare materiel.

The army has been disposing of chemical weapons for years and has an outstanding record of safety. It uses high-quality filters, computerized monitoring systems, and the latest scientific designs to incinerate weapons. The military makes the country safer by incinerating these dangerous weapons before an accident seriously harms the surrounding community.

Since 1990, the U.S. Army has used incineration safely and successfully to dispose of the country's stockpile of chemical nerve and blister agents. To date, more than one million chemical weapons and more than 12 million pounds of chemical agent has been destroyed.

The Johnston Atoll Chemical Agent Disposal System (JACADS) began incineration operations in 1990 and destroyed its last chemical agent munition in November 2000. The Army has an incineration facility operating in Utah, facilities preparing for operations in Alabama and Oregon and a facility under construction in Arkansas.

The chemical weapons disposal facilities are state-of-the-

U.S. Army Chemical Materials Agency, "Incineration: A Safe, Proven Disposal Process," www.cma.army.mil, June 4, 2004.

art, engineered with specially designed weapons handling processes, remote-controlled incineration and disposal equipment, complex control systems and detailed procedures and training to protect the workers, environment and public.

> *The Army's incineration processes are based on years of experience and advances that ensure safe disposal of the various nerve and blister agents, munitions and containers.*

The Army's incineration processes are based on years of experience and advances that ensure safe disposal of the various nerve and blister agents, munitions and containers. The Environmental Protection Agency publicly stated that emissions from JACADS are the cleanest of any incinerator in the United States.

Safety Features

The Army's incineration process includes the following safety features:

• *Stringent emission standards.* The Army monitors incinerator stack emissions at levels much stricter than regulatory standards. In turn, the regulatory standards are much lower than amounts that could cause public health problems. Monitoring at higher levels than required demonstrates the Army's commitment to safe operations. In addition, these monitoring levels were established with the assistance and approval of the Department of Health and Human Services' Centers for Disease Control and the Surgeon General's Office.

• *Higher temperatures to ensure complete agent destruction.* Army incinerators operate at significantly higher temperatures and longer periods of time than commercial hazardous waste incinerators. This ensures complete destruction of chemical agent and total decontamination of the casings and munition pieces.

Gases from the incinerator furnaces pass through a pollution abatement or removal system to further cleanse emissions. As a final safeguard, the emissions are monitored to ensure complete destruction of agent.

• *Automatic shutdown if irregularities are detected.* Computer programs in the control system monitor the process for such things as incinerator temperatures, airflow rates and pressures. These programs automatically shut down the feeding of agent to the incinerators if process irregularities are detected. Agent processing is not restarted until corrective actions have been taken and approved by oversight agencies.

• *Additional safety features.* Other safety features of the incineration facilities include:

- Air pressure inside the facility is lower than outside air pressure. Air is drawn from outside the facility through the outer rooms and into the most toxic areas. Air from the toxic areas is drawn out of the plant through a series of charcoal filters. This ensures that agent vapors are contained and that only clean ventilation air is released to the environment.
- Explosives and rocket propellants are removed or processed only in special automated explosion containment rooms designed to contain an unlikely explosion.
- Agent is drained from the munitions into storage tanks until it is incinerated. The storage tanks are designed to contain the chemical agent in the event of an earthquake.

Lessons Learned

The Army has a formal lessons learned program to collect improvements made at one site and ensure they are considered for use at all disposal sites. Lessons learned while operating the first disposal plant have benefited the other facilities. These benefits include special equipment and handling procedures for chemical landmines, techniques for dealing with unusual conditions caused by deteriorating chemical weapons, techniques for working in protective equipment and overall design and process improvements. . . .

The incineration processes are backed by years of experience and have been scrutinized closely by the public; local, state and federal government officials; . . . oversight agencies; and the court systems. To date, incineration is the only full-scale technology demonstrated in real-time operations to safely treat the complete munition—agent, explosives, metal pieces and packaging material.

3

The Military Should Not Be Exempt from Hazardous Waste Rules

Jon R. Luoma

Jon R. Luoma is a journalist who writes for Mother Jones *and is the author of* Hidden Forest: The Biography of an Ecosystem.

The U.S. military has been contaminating the environment for decades. Millions of acres of land on military bases are littered with nuclear waste, chemical poisons, bioweapons, and hazardous solid debris such as lead munitions. Although the poisons are contaminating the air and water in surrounding communities, the Pentagon is lobbying Congress for exemption from environmental laws. After years of poisoning the land, air, and water, the Pentagon should not be allowed to walk away from the messes it has created.

"It feels like somebody wrote a new rule—the bigger a mess you make, the easier it should be to just walk away," says Laura Olah, a Wisconsin activist who heads a grassroots group called Citizens for Safe Water Around Badger. Badger, in this case, is a former Army ammunition plant near the town of Sauk Prairie, Wisconsin—a sprawling industrial complex that operated from World War II through the mid-1970s and produced not only munitions, but a flood of toxic wastes. Today, a witches' brew of contaminants, including the heavy metals mercury and cadmium and the cancer-causing compounds carbon tetrachloride and trichloroethylene, is seeping into the groundwater beneath the 7,300-acre site. For more than a decade, several local farm families unwittingly drew their well water directly from the heart of the contamination; in the nearby Wisconsin River, sediments are contaminated with more than 20 times the allowable amount of mercury.

Olah says her group just wants the Defense Department to clean up the site before it abandons Badger entirely. But the Pentagon has missed a series of deadlines in a cleanup agreement with the state of Wisconsin. In recent years, it has also backed away from a plan to remove large volumes of contaminated soil from the base, proposing instead to fence off and monitor the toxic hot spots.

Badger is hardly an isolated case. From Cape Cod in Massachusetts to McClellan Air Force Base in California, the Pentagon is facing mounting criticism for failing to clean up military sites contaminated with everything from old munitions to radioactive materials and residues from biological-weapons research. Now, citing the demands of the war on terrorism and working with sympathetic officials in the administration and Congress, the department has stepped up efforts to remove substantial parts of its operations from environmental oversight.

A Disturbing Trend

Last December [2002], Defense officials drew up a 24-page strategy memorandum, laying out a plan for a "multi-year campaign" to exempt the military from federal laws including the Marine Mammal Protection Act, the Endangered Species Act, and the Clean Air Act, as well as rules governing solid and hazardous wastes. The strategy also called for Congress to state "that munitions deposited and remaining on operational ranges are not 'solid wastes'"—a move that with one stroke would exempt the Pentagon from having to clean up the old shells, fuels, and other weapons "constituents" that turn places like Badger into health hazards.

The Pentagon is seeking these changes even though current law already allows it to gain exemptions from any environmental regulations that might hinder military preparedness; according to a 2002 study by Congress' General Accounting Office, the Defense Department has never run into any significant problems in this regard.

Nonetheless, Bush appointees at the EPA [Environmental

Protection Agency] appear to have embraced the Pentagon's agenda. In April [2003], EPA enforcement chief John Suarez told Congress that the Pentagon's proposals to ease hazardous-waste regulations were "appropriate" and in line with "existing EPA policy"—even though only weeks earlier, a report from Suarez's own staff to the President's Office of Management and Budget had specifically warned against relaxing the waste rules, noting that the munitions could present "an imminent and substantial endangerment of health or the environment." The hazardous-waste exemption failed to pass Congress [in 2003]—though the Pentagon got one step closer to an item on its environmental wish list when the House approved an exemption to the Marine Mammal Protection Act, which has been an impediment to a controversial Navy sonar program [that is said to harm whales and other marine Life]. Hill staffers say they expect the hazardous-waste proposal to be introduced again in the coming months.

> **" *Nearly half the 206 sites studied lacked adequate fencing, or even simple signs, to keep the public away from areas where hazardous munitions might lie.* "**

The changes could affect thousands of sites across the nation. Late last year [2002], EPA staffers prepared an internal briefing document for Suarez, suggesting that removing toxic waste just from the Pentagon's thousands of weapons ranges "has the potential to be the largest environmental cleanup program ever to be implemented in the United States." According to the report, which was never publicly released, the contaminated ranges cover an area as large as Florida, or about 40 million acres. Yet, it noted, there had been a "disturbing trend" on the Pentagon's part of taking "ill-advised short-cuts to limit costs."

Threats to Human Health

In all, more than 27,000 military waste sites have been documented nationwide; they include the vast Massachusetts Military Reservation on Cape Cod, where contamination threatens the drinking water for more than a quarter million residents, as well as Fort Detrick in Maryland, where cleanup contractors in 2001 turned up test tubes filled with residues of anthrax and other bioweapons materials. But even as the scope of the problem continues to expand, internal EPA reports suggest, the Department of Defense is seeking to conceal the extent of the contamination.

> *They're casting [environmental exemptions] as an issue of military readiness in the age of terrorism, and leaning hard on everyone . . . to get out of the way.*

According to a survey of inactive weapons ranges commissioned by the Pentagon in 2000, nearly half the 206 sites studied lacked adequate fencing, or even simple signs, to keep the public away from areas where hazardous munitions might lie. The same report also found that wastes from chemical or biological weapons might be present at more than 50 percent of the sites. The document's first draft stopped just short of calling the Defense Department a scofflaw, stating that it "often does not adhere to . . . applicable statutes or regulations" and concluding that "the ranges in this survey pose potentially significant threats to human health and the environment."

By the time the final version of the report appeared later that year, both of those statements, along with seven additional pages of observations and criticisms of the Pentagon, had been removed. Jeff Ruch, executive director of Public Employees for Environmental Responsibility—a whistleblower group that obtained copies of the original document—says agency staffers told him that the report had been censored in response to pressure from the Pentagon.

In recent months, the Pentagon has quietly scored a series of other concessions from the EPA. In one decision—announced in a press release late on a Friday last July [2003]—the agency declared that it would not, as had been widely expected, tighten drinking-water standards for perchlorate, a rocket-fuel additive that has contaminated scores of bases and weapons-manufacturing sites. Perchlorate seeping into the Colorado River from a Nevada rocket plant has contaminated the drinking-water supply for 15 million people; a recent study by the nonprofit Environmental Working Group suggests that most of the nation's winter lettuce—the bulk of which is irrigated with Colorado River water—contains significant amounts of the toxin.

[In the summer of 2003], the EPA announced it would no longer require property owners to remove polychlorinated biphenyls (PCBs), which are also suspected carcinogens, from buildings before selling them—a change that would largely benefit the Pentagon, which owns hundreds of PCB-contaminated sites. Under the new rules, the Pentagon could transfer those sites to schools, hospitals, and other civilian users without incurring liability for the contamination or requiring evidence of any cleanup.

Watchdog groups expect the Defense Department to continue pushing for environmental exemptions, both within the administration and in Congress. "This isn't over," says Karen Wayland of the Washington-based Natural Resources Defense Council. "There was such a public outcry when they first floated these ideas a couple of years ago that we thought they'd back off. But they're casting it as an issue of military readiness in the age of terrorism, and leaning hard on everyone from the moderate Republicans in Congress to the EPA to get out of the way."

4

The Environmental Justice Movement Fights Corporate Polluting in Minority Neighborhoods

Eddie J. Girdner and Jack Smith

Eddie J. Girdner teaches international relations at Baskent University in Turkey and is the author of People and Power: An Introduction to Politics. *Jack Smith is a journalist who teaches English and philosophy at North Central Missouri College.*

In the past ten years the environmental justice movement, or EJM, has united low-income women, Native Americans, African Americans, Hispanics, and other minority groups to fight pollution in their communities. While the struggle against corporations that pollute their communities is often long and difficult, the environmental justice movement can resist environmental racism. By coming together to fight hazardous waste, pollution, and other toxic nightmares, communities can save their health, their children, and their neighborhoods.

M any communities [have] become sacrifice zones for the dumping of the enormous amounts of toxics produced through production techniques that enhance profits. Clearly, environmental policies of governments and corporations have targeted the weak in American society. This is quite evident in the frequently cited 1984 report of Cerrell Associates to the California Waste Management Board. In the report, entitled *Political Difficulties Facing Waste-to-Energy Conversion Plant Siting*, the conclusion reads: "All socioeconomic groupings tend to resent the nearby siting of major facilities, but middle and upper socioeconomic status possess better resources to effectuate their opposition. Middle and higher socioeconomic strata neighborhoods should not fall within the one-mile and five-mile radius of the proposed site." Target communities should include those under 25,000 population, be rural, politically conservative, free market orientated, above middle age, with high school or less education, farmers, miners, those with low income, and those who are likely to see significant economic benefits in the waste industry for the local community.

> *Through active involvement in [environmental] groups, people of color, women, and members of working-class communities . . . develop leadership skills.*

The environmental justice movement [EMJ] emerged in the 1990s in the United States as part of the grassroots environmental struggle by community activists fighting any number of toxic battles. The term "environmental justice" itself emerged from the work of antitoxics activists, especially in the South. The EJM linked the issue of social, economic, and political marginalization of women, minorities, and poor communities to environmental issues such as toxic pollution, the right to a clean environment, and workplace hazards. The EJM can be traced back to the 1960s Civil Rights Movement, urban disturbances over uncollected garbage, and to the Memphis sanitation workers' strike in 1968. This movement, with over 7,000 community grassroots groups nationwide, has expanded grassroots democratic environmentalism in minority and economically depressed communities and raised the awareness of environmental racism and class discrimination.

The major issues of the EJM include toxics, waste facility siting, urban industrial pollution, childhood lead poisoning,

farm workers and pesticides, land rights, sustainable development, export of toxics to the Global South, risky technology,
and leaking landfills (which include virtually all landfills). The
EJM has also led to demands for a superfund for workers, restrictions on capital flight, elimination of production of toxic
substances, less-polluting transportation systems, environmentally sound economic development, equitable distribution of
cleanup programs, international laws that protect the environment and worker rights, and justice for the poor in countries of
the Global South.

The environmental justice movement is a broad, comprehensive movement for social justice, organized around profes-
sional networks of organizations, such as the Citizens Clearinghouse on Hazardous Waste (later changed to the Center for
Health, Environment and Justice), the African American Environmental Association, the Southwest Organizing Project, the
Southwest Network for Environmental and Economic Justice,
the Southern Organizing Committee for Economic and Social
Justice, the Gulf Coast Tenants Association, the African-
American Black and Green Tendency in California, and many
others. It is multiracial and multiethnic, uniting African Americans, other ethnic groups, women, and low-income communities around environmental justice issues. Robert D. Bullard
points out that the EJM is characterized by grassroots activism
and is a bottom-up movement. This suggests that minority communities have always been interested in environmental issues
but were previously excluded from the mainstream movement.
These grassroots groups serve as information centers for the assistance of local environmental groups all across the country.

> ❝ *The weakest sections of the society confront
> some of the most powerful forces, such as huge
> corporations and governments and their flocks of
> highly paid, high-flying lawyers.* ❞

Environmental justice groups often emerge from organization and mobilization around a single issue and move on to
multi-issue agendas as they network with other groups. Local
groups conduct their own research in their own communities
to challenge the experts and demand roles in decision making

about issues which directly affect their lives. Through active involvement in such groups, people of color, women, and members of working-class communities gain opportunities to develop leadership skills and to share their experiences with other grassroots groups.

> *I believed in democracy, but then I discovered that it was government and industry that abused my rights.*

The environmental justice movement has not only brought African Americans, Mexican Americans, Native Americans, women, and low-income white individuals into the environmental movement, it has succeeded in putting the agenda for environmental justice on the national public agenda. After a series of national studies and conferences, such as the First National People of Color Environmental Leadership Conference in 1991 in Washington, D.C., and conferences at the University of Michigan School of Natural Resources, activists made demands directly to national officials for action. In 1992, the EPA created the Office of Environmental Justice, and on February 11, 1993, President Clinton signed Executive Order 12898, which directs federal agencies to incorporate environmental justice principles as part of day-to-day operations. Grassroots groups work to hold the government accountable for policy actions and demand policies that actually result in the improvement of the environmental health of communities and protect the people who live there. Mainstream environmental groups, such as the Sierra Club, the Wilderness Society, and the Conservation Foundation, were pressured to diversify their leadership from their mostly white male staffs.

The EJM embraces both liberal reform, at one end of the spectrum, and radical demands for an alternative economic system at the other. Radical groups may challenge the fundamental social, economic, and political structures and institutions of the U.S. and global political economy, which are believed to contribute to inequality and injustice for minority and low-income communities. Such inequality is evident in toxic pollution of air and water, increased sickness and disease, increased incidence of cancer, deteriorating communities, and

unsafe workplaces for the politically weak. For radical environmentalists, the quest for development, even if viewed as "sustainable development" and "progress," puts a disproportionate
share of the costs on minority and low-income communities
and is at the root of the present national and global environmental crisis. This situation can only worsen if corporate ex-
ploitation of the earth's resources is not challenged by a different pattern of development of communities that puts people
before profits, empowers people to make decisions that protect
their livelihood, and ensures a healthy environment and future
for the children of all groups and classes in society.

At the beginning of the new century, one of the most press-
ing issues continues to be waste, both in the form of household
solid waste and hazardous waste. EJM struggles continue to re-
volve around solid and hazardous waste landfills, solid and
hazardous waste incineration, the increasing use of hazardous
wastes as fuels for cement kilns and other industrial purposes,
the rail and barge shipments of solid waste for hundreds of
miles into local communities, and other environmental in-
equities. Atmospheric toxics and cleanup of old industrial sites
in urban slums are salient issues for both big corporations and
EJM activists.

The right to know the environmental record of companies
is also an issue under resistance from corporations. Corporate
secrecy laws suggest that the power of monopoly capital is a
greater threat than ever to people struggling to hold onto their
democratic rights. Various means of hollowing out the power
of local governments, under the concept of "preemption,"
have made EJM struggles more and more problematic.

EJM Struggles

Celene Krauss has attempted to understand the participation of
blue-collar women in the EJM in terms of ideas from feminist
writings and new social historiography. Krauss argues that these
approaches provide theoretical perspectives that are helpful in
understanding the emergence of grassroots environmental political struggles, more broadly. Five key mechanisms are at work:
First, there is the emergence of a critical political consciousness
in practice, or, more specifically, in confrontation with the industry, state, and political power complex. Second, as a result,
there is increasing understanding of the link between private
encroachment and public power. Third, the emergence of a po-

litical struggle grounded in popular culture and the perception that deeply held traditions and values are being violated. Fourth, the loss of community and livelihood with the encroaching intervention of the state and the market. Fifth, the emergence of a strong leadership role by marginalized peoples such as minorities, women, Native Americans, and the poor. Women are concerned about the health of their children as well as the broader community.

> *Women are particularly important in EJM struggles because . . . women tend to be more willing to challenge the system when it threatens their children's health.*

The dynamics of EJM struggles certainly bear out the profile Krauss offers here. The weakest sections of the society confront some of the most powerful forces, such as huge corporations and governments and their flocks of highly paid, high-flying lawyers. These struggles tend to have a David and Goliath character about them. Environmentalists are forced to depend upon free legal defense from lawyers who sympathize with their cause. State intervention may become the "kiss of death." On the other hand, the state can sometimes assist, when environmentalists force the state to obey its own laws. The state may play a positive role in environmental struggles, for example, in closing landfills that are polluting the groundwater and shutting down waste incinerators that are threatening people's health. More often than not, however, the political, economic, and legal structures militate against environmental and health concerns. Politicians know they cannot win elections without the campaign money from the most polluting corporations in their states. Economic growth and corporate profits tend to be the bottom line.

When confronted with such a challenge, people develop a critical consciousness. This insight begins to "unmask" the ideology of popular participation and democracy. Political consciousness arises and is continuously molded from the everyday world of experience. People expect the political process to work for them, assuming that their elected public officials are on their side. As Lois Gibbs wrote, "I believed in democracy, but then I discovered that it was government and industry that abused my rights. But my experience is not unique." When people discover that government and industry are working against their interests, which happens often in environmental struggles, their political consciousness is heightened. Their struggle also "unmasks" the ideology that hides the relationship between their private lives and public policies. In environmental struggles, those at the margins of society usually find that they are expendable, to be made sacrifices for the more powerful, the industrial culture, and "progress," under the guise of "economic development."

Grassroots struggle is a process whereby those on the periphery of the society and economy confront those at the center, the owners and decision makers. Those on the periphery tend to be women, minorities, rural residents, Native Americans, and the poorest segments of society. In other words, those marginalized politically and economically. Since these marginalized elements—the average person, in Walter Lippmann's words—are supposed to listen to the managerial class in American society, their entry into the political process is often seen as deeply subversive of the prevailing and established political process in the United States. It is. They challenge business as usual, whereby the corporations run the economy, and business is carried out through the relatively controlled process of elections, courts, legislation, and so on. For example, it is clear that in many cases, public hearings on environmental matters are not meant to affect the procedure of approval or disapproval of projects; this process primarily serves to allow the public to let off steam. However, the system operates within an ideology that claims that democracy exists, but this belief has not actually been put to the litmus test for most people until they are involved in a struggle that directly threatens their health, lifestyle, and community.

Women as Activists

As struggles emerge, the movement grows out of popular culture, traditions and community. This process has been called "cultural activism." The debate is very much alive as to what elements such movements are rooted in. Tradition, local economics, culture, religious traditions, ethnic values, local customs, family and individual circumstances all may play a role. Local cultures differ widely even within the same state in the

United States, and within different regions of the community. To some extent, it may be a matter of how dominant the state and market have become. Human activity in the periphery may be driven less by market incentives and other pecuniary factors. In rural cultures, farmers may come to see a link between ecology and their rural farming culture. . . .

> *// Environmental racism is the unequal protection against toxic and hazardous waste exposure and the systematic exclusion of people of color from environmental decisions affecting communities. //*

Women are particularly important in EJM struggles because beyond the influence of the traditional culture, women tend to be more willing to challenge the system when it threatens their children's health. It has been noted that 70 to 80 percent of the local leaders who challenge the system are women. They are often seen as "emotional housewives" but actually "derive power from their emotionality." In EJM struggles, especially toxic struggles, women generally participate more than men.

Indeed, women have played a disproportionately important role in the EJM. Scholars have noted that "[W]omen have been at the forefront of every historical and political movement to reclaim the earth." Housewives with no previous leadership experience have taken the lead in fighting toxics in the United States. Many have become nationally known figures, among them Crystal Eastman, Alice Hamilton, and Florence Kelley, who pioneered research on workplace hazards. Rachel Carson, Lois Gibbs, Penny Newman, Kaye Kiker, Cora Tucker, and Helen Caldicott are among the leading activists against hazardous wastes in their local communities and are also nationally known among environmental activists in the United States. In East Livermore, Ohio, local housewife Terri Swearingen led the fight against a hazardous waste incinerator; the struggle still continues while the incinerator burns. In Jacksonville, Arkansas, Patty Frase organized the Arkansas Clean-up Alliance. Both of her parents died after the Vertac Chemical plant burned TCDD dioxin. A Louisiana woman, Emelda West, from Convent, Louisiana, traveled to Japan to the headquarters of Shin-Etsu Chemical Company to fight against the building of a chemical plant that would emit up to 450,000 pounds of toxic fumes a year. These women have emerged as key figures in their communities to lead the fight against existing and proposed facilities. They have organized their communities and networked across the nation sharing information and tactics. They have become political leaders too in demanding changes in the law and the system. As one Missouri woman put it, they "get in the face" of those who control the system.

When women take the bull by the horns, this assertiveness "helps define a new source of community." Antitoxics movements often become community development movements whereby new community leaders, often women, emerge. In this way, the issue of who should be leaders in the movement and in the community is raised and dealt with. In such movements, women do not merely participate; they lead, often pulling in the men too.

African American Activism

Racial inequality among communities in terms of environmental pollution and quality of life is well documented in the environmental justice literature. According to Bunyan Bryant, environmental racism "refers to those institutional rules, regulations and policies of government or corporate decisions that deliberately target certain communities for least desirable land uses, resulting in the disproportionate exposure of toxic and hazardous waste on communities based upon certain prescribed biological characteristics. Environmental racism is the unequal protection against toxic and hazardous waste exposure and the systematic exclusion of people of color from environmental decisions affecting communities."

A U.S. General Accounting Office (GAO) report in 1983 stated that of hazardous waste landfill communities in the U.S., three-quarters are poor, African American, or Latino-American. The *National Law Journal* staff reported that "penalties under hazardous waste laws at sites having the greatest white population were about 500 percent higher than the penalties at sites with the greatest minority population, averaging $335,566 for white areas, compared to $55,318 for minority areas. . . . For all the federal environmental laws aimed at protecting citizens from air, water, and waste pollution, penalties in white communities were 46 percent higher than in minority communities. Under the giant Superfund cleanup program, abandoned hazardous waste sites in minority areas take 20 percent longer to be placed on the national priority list than those in white areas. In more than half of the 10 autonomous regions that administer EPA programs around the country, action on cleanup at Superfund sites begins from 12 percent to 42 percent later at minority sites than at white sites. At the minority sites, the EPA chooses 'containment,' the capping or walling off of a hazardous dump site, 7 percent more frequently than the cleanup method preferred under the law of permanent 'treatment,' to eliminate the waste or rid it of its toxins. At white sites, the EPA orders treatment 22 percent more often than containment."

The Federal Agency for Toxic Substances Registry found that for families earning less than $6,000 annually, 68 percent of African American children had lead poisoning, compared with 36 percent for white children. In families with an annual income of over $15,000, more than 38 percent of African American children suffer from lead poisoning, compared with 12 percent of white children. In Los Angeles, over 71 percent of African Americans and 50 percent of Latino Americans live in communities within the most polluted area, compared with only 34 percent of whites in such polluted communities.

A well-known study by the Commission for Racial Justice found race to be the most important factor in the location of toxic waste sites. Three out of five African Americans live in communities with abandoned toxic-waste sites. Most hazardous waste incineration takes place in minority communities. There are many other findings that document this racial inequality. . . .

Ultimately, "achieving environmental justice demands major restructuring of the entire social order" [according to John Belamy Foster]. Such restructuring would include a challenge to absolute property rights; a challenge to the logic of growth without limit; the right of everyone to a clean environment; the concept of security as a sustainable ecological system, rather than military superiority; and social planning and grassroots democracy as the basis for environmentally sound growth. There must be a shift of power from corporate public policy making to local policy making by the people. After all, heads of corporations are not elected by the people. Nevertheless, they run totalitarian organizations that affect thousands and even millions of people's lives. The New Right ideology, from ideologues such as Frederick Hayek, which sanctifies and deifies private property, effectively serves as the groundwork for the emerging dictatorship of the corporatariat. . . . The EJM often involves a major shift in the concept of democracy as it has existed in American society—from traditional elite to grassroots democracy. People must have the right to know about health effects of toxics, the right to inspect facilities, and the right to negotiate agreements with responsible parties.

5

The Environmental Justice Movement Is Preventing Economic Growth in Minority Neighborhoods

FreedomWorks

FreedomWorks, led by former senators Dick Armey and Jack Kemp, is a conservative organization that works to have taxes lowered and government regulation on business reduced.

Members of the environmental justice movement claim that minority neighborhoods are often targeted as sites for toxic waste dumps and polluting factories. They also say that minorities suffer a higher proportion of cancer and other diseases as a result. Scientific studies have shown that these claims are untrue and that middle-class neighborhoods are just as likely to be affected by pollution. By preventing industry from locating to inner-city neighborhoods, the environmental justice movement is actually discriminating against the poor who need factory jobs to help them escape poverty.

For the sake of so-called environmental justice, the Environmental Protection Agency (EPA) [enacted in 1994] barriers to much-needed economic growth in low-income and minority communities. Supporters of "environmental justice" claim that such communities have been unfairly targeted with polluting industries and waste disposal sites. They allege that such communities also receive lower priority for hazardous waste cleanups than wealthy, non-minority communities. As a result, they claim, there are far more outbreaks of cancer and other diseases among minority and low-income families than in the rest of society.

> *Researchers . . . found that hazardous-waste sites are 'no more likely to be located in [neighborhoods] with higher percentages of blacks and Hispanics.'*

Environmental justice supporters want Americans to believe that a large number of studies support their claims, and they have convinced many policymakers that using the Civil Rights Act of 1964 to shut down economic development is the only remedy. Government should not create new barriers to economic growth in communities where it is most needed.

A Real Threat?

Scientists and statisticians who have studied the issue found that environmental justice has little or no basis in fact. Researchers at the University of Massachusetts found that hazardous-waste sites are "no more likely to be located in [neighborhoods] with higher percentages of blacks and Hispanics than in other [neighborhoods]." A study by the University of Chicago called environmental justice "garbage" and found that in the Chicago area, middle-class, nonminorities are more likely to live near dumps and toxic waste sites than minorities and low-income Americans. Another study found that in many cases, landfills and waste incinerators in minority neighborhoods had been built long before the areas became populated by minorities.

Environmental justice supporters also claim that hazardous-waste sites are cleaned up faster in wealthy communities with few minorities. However, the study upon which this claim is based had "serious methodological problems" according to Bernard R. Siskin, a Ph.D. statistician who actually worked for the EPA. Moreover, there is no reliable evidence that minorities and low-income Americans develop pollution-related illnesses more often than anyone else.

Costly Barriers

In 1994, President Clinton issued Executive Order 12898 instructing each cabinet agency to make "achieving environmental justice part of its mission." Because of this order, the EPA has deemed that almost anyone can shut down a development project within six months of federal permits being issued simply by claiming that the project violates Title VI of the Civil Rights Act of 1964.

The potential cost of so-called environmental justice policies to all citizens—but especially to minorities and low-income Americans—is devastating. If environmental justice supporters have their way, a surge of lawsuits will clog the courts while economic development and job creation in low-income and minority communities is stifled. As Detroit's Mayor Dennis Archer has stated: "The redevelopment of Detroit and urban areas could be chilled by the federal government's 'environmental justice' policies." In Louisiana, plans for two factories worth $700 million and $800 million, along with hundreds of jobs, were cancelled due to "environmental justice."

Even more tragic is the fact that when scarce dollars are wasted on "environmental justice," real environmental and health risks to low-income and minority communities—such as lead paint exposure, inadequate prenatal care, diabetes, asthma, substance abuse, and violence—are neglected.

> *There is no reliable evidence that minorities and low-income Americans develop pollution-related illnesses more often than anyone else.*

In fact, the states have felt these concerns so strongly that in March 1998, the Environmental Council of the States (ECOS), which represents 49 of the 50 state environmental agencies, passed a resolution calling upon the EPA to end its destructive environmental justice policies.

Focusing on non-existent problems like environmental justice will do nothing to bring investment into neighborhoods in desperate need of opportunities. Government should not get in the way of the creation of jobs and wealth in low-income and minority communities. If the federal government is truly concerned about these communities, it should scrap regulations that prevent the development of former industrial sites known as "brownfields," and fundamentally reform the Superfund law[1] to speed the cleanup of toxic waste sites in urban areas.

Supporters of environmental justice should focus their energy on removing barriers to economic growth and solving real health problems instead of creating a quota system for prosperity.

1. The Comprehensive Environmental Response, Compensation, and Liability Act or "Superfund" was created in 1980 to clean up abandoned hazardous waste sites, chemical spills, accidents, and emergency releases of toxins into the environment.

6

The Chemical Industry Is Exposing People to Toxic Substances

Stacy Malkan

*Stacy Malkan is a journalist and the communications direc-
tor for Health Care Without Harm, an international coalition of hospitals and health care systems, medical profes-
sionals, and community groups dedicated to transforming
the health care industry so that it is ecologically sustainable.*

With the chemical industry annually dumping billions
of pounds of toxic chemicals on the land and in the air
and water, the human body has become a toxic waste
zone. Recent studies show that the average American
carries at least fifty industrial chemicals in his or her
body. Most of these toxins are known carcinogens and
there can be little doubt that they are harming human
health, especially that of children. Because the government has not acquired tests on the effects of these substances on the human body, chemical corporations
have been allowed to use American citizens as guinea
pigs while producing massive quantities of hazardous
waste. It is time for industries to start behaving as responsible corporate citizens. They need to make people's
health as high a priority as profits and stop producing
dozens of carcinogenic chemicals.

C hemical contamination of water, air and food supplies has
been documented for decades, but only recently have sci-

entists begun to uncover details about the industrial pollution of a much more intimate site: our bodies.

It should come as no surprise that industrial chemicals are running through our veins. Industry reported dumping 7.1 billion pounds of hazardous compounds into the air and water in the United States in the year 2000, according to the most recent Toxic Release Inventory, a U.S. Environmental Protection Agency (EPA) program that tracks only a subset of industries.

But not until recently, with advances in the technology of biomonitoring, have scientists been able to accurately measure the actual levels of chemicals in people's bodies.

Now, with the recent release of the largest-ever biomonitoring study by the U.S. Centers for Disease Control and Prevention (CDC), and a new peer-reviewed study by independent researchers, scientists know more than they ever have about a new evolutionary phenomenon: the universal chemical body burden of people.

"This is irrefutable proof that humans carry around scores of industrial chemicals, most of which have never been tested for human health effects," says Jane Houlihan, vice president of research at the Washington D.C.–based Environmental Working Group (EWG), and lead author of one of the studies.

Most of these chemicals did not exist in the environment, let alone in human bodies, just 75 years ago.

The $450-billion chemical industry has responded with assurances that the mere presence of chemicals in people is no proof of harm, but critics say the human population is the unwitting test subject of a dangerous and unprecedented chemical experiment.

Chemical Load

The . . . CDC National Report on Human Exposure to Environmental Chemicals, released in January [2003], is the largest set of body burden data ever collected in the U.S. and the first time chemical exposure by age, race and sex has been analyzed on a national scale. CDC tested the blood and urine of a nationally representative group of Americans for the presence of 116 toxic chemicals—all of which were found in people.

"This report is by far the most extensive assessment ever made of the exposure in the U.S. population to environmental chemicals," says CDC Deputy Director Dr. David Fleming. "It's a quantum leap forward in providing objective scientific information about what's getting into people's bodies and how much."

Public health experts say one of the most disturbing findings is that children had higher body burdens than adults of some of the most toxic chemicals, including lead, tobacco smoke and organophosphate pesticides.

"This is a concern because of the potential of toxic chemicals to interfere with development," says Dr. Lynn Goldman, a former EPA official and a professor at the Johns Hopkins University School of Public Health.

> // *Children had higher body burdens . . . of the most toxic chemicals, including lead, tobacco smoke and organophosphate pesticides.* //

Children had double the level of adults of the pesticide chlorpyrifos (known as Dursban)—a chemical that animal studies indicate has long-term effects on brain development if exposure occurs early in life. Dursban was the most widely used insecticide in the United States until the EPA banned its use in households [in 2002], although some uses remain legal. Other organophosphate pesticides, also linked to neurological and nervous system damage in animal studies, remain in widespread use.

Children were also disproportionately exposed to some of the most toxic phthalates, the CDC found. Phthalates—a class of industrial chemicals used in polyvinyl chloride (PVC) plastic, cosmetics and other consumer products—cause a spectrum of health effects in animal studies, including damage to the liver, kidneys, lungs and the reproductive system, particularly the testes of developing males.

CDC also identified some spikes among ethnic populations. The insecticide DDT, banned in the 1970s in the United States, was found in Mexican Americans at triple the levels present in the general population.

CDC found mercury at the highest levels in African-American women of childbearing age, and the study confirmed that 5 to 10 percent of all U.S. women of childbearing age already have enough mercury in their bodies to pose a risk of neurological damage to their developing babies.

CDC plans to release more body burden data every two

years, including more information about potential sources of mercury, phthalates and other chemicals of particular concern.

Fifty or More Chemicals

If the CDC report provides a panoramic view of the body burden of the U.S. population, another new study by the Environmental Working Group released in January [2003] offers a close-up snapshot at what individuals are carrying around in their bodies.

EWG looked for 210 chemicals in nine people and created a personal body burden profile for each—putting a human face, as well as a corporate face, on the problem.

Using peer-reviewed studies and various government health assessments, the report links the chemicals to potential health effects and found that, on average, each person's body had 50 or more chemicals that are linked to cancer in humans or lab animals, considered toxic to the brain and nervous system, associated with birth defects or abnormal development, or known to interfere with the hormone system.

The report also connected the chemicals to 11,700 consumer products, and to 164 past and current manufacturers.

So the study showed, for example, that Andrea Martin, 56, of Sausalito, California, contained at least 95 toxic chemicals in her body at the time of the test, which she likely ingested from scores of consumer products that are manufactured by Shell, Union Carbide, Exxon, Dow and Monsanto, among others.

"I was shocked at the breadth and variety of the number of chemicals. I was outraged to find out that without my permission, without my knowledge, my body was accumulating this toxic mixture," Martin says.

> *I was outraged to find out that without my permission, without my knowledge, my body was accumulating this toxic mixture.*

Martin appeared in a full-page ad announcing the body burden report that ran in the *New York Times* in January [2003]. Her photo was stamped with the headline: "Warning: Andrea Martin contains 59 cancer causing industrial chemicals."

She also happens to have cancer. At 42, Martin was diagnosed with an advanced case of breast cancer, underwent aggressive treatment and later contracted cancer in the other breast. A year ago, she was diagnosed with a large malignant brain tumor.

"My body biology is susceptible to cancer," Martin surmises. She has been asked if she thinks her chemical body burden caused the disease. "No one can say for sure, but no one can say it hasn't either," she says. "We deserve to know what toxins are in our bodies. We have a right to know what health effects these chemicals have."

Never Evaluated for Health Effects

Unfortunately, for everything scientists now know about which chemicals are in the environment and in people, there is much more they don't know about the effects on human health.

"Just because a chemical can be measured doesn't mean it causes disease," says Dr. Richard Jackson, director of the CDC's National Center for Environmental Health. The new CDC data offers "no new health effects information, no new understanding of the health effects from chemicals," Jackson says. "But it moves the science forward to increase this understanding."

The majority of people in the United States mistakenly believe that the government tests chemicals used in consumer products to make sure they are safe, according to an opinion poll recently conducted by the Washington Toxics Coalition.

The chemical industry also makes public claims to that effect. "Chemicals are evaluated by government scientists before being used, and there are precautions in place to help keep us safe from both natural toxins and modern chemicals," said a statement of the American Chemistry Council (ACC), the trade group for the biggest chemical manufacturers, issued in response to the CDC study.

However, most of the 75,000-plus chemicals in use today have never been evaluated for health effects. Most industrial chemicals in use today are regulated by the minimal health and safety standards of the Toxic Substances Control Act (TSCA), which assumes chemicals are safe until they are proven hazardous. TSCA does not require chemical companies to conduct health or safety studies prior to putting a chemical on the market, or to monitor chemicals once they are in use.

EWG accuses the chemical industry of creating the lax regulatory situation. "Chemical companies are pressuring our elected leaders to restrict new research and block common sense safeguards," says the *New York Times* ad paid for by the environmental group.

The ACC blasted the ad as an attempt to "put bogus words in the mouths of the men and women who make essential and life-saving products that we rely on every day" and said that "chemical makers support additional government research and also are spending millions of dollars every year in collaboration with government scientists on research into the relationship between chemicals and health."

Industry points to its voluntary efforts to improve health and safety performance, and says that significant reductions in chemical releases have occurred under the Responsible Care program, a voluntary program established by the ACC in 1988 in response to criticism of industry's environmental record.

But a recent study by Duke University associate professor Michael Lenox found that some members of Responsible Care are releasing more toxic substances into the environment than non-members, prompting Lenox to criticize the voluntary program as a failure.

In responding to the CDC report, industry has focused on the small levels of chemicals detected by biomonitoring. "It is remarkable that modern chemistry allows CDC scientists to measure incredibly small amounts of certain nutrients, natural food chemicals and modern chemicals in our bodies," says the ACC.

> *The majority of people in the United States mistakenly believe that the government tests chemicals used in consumer products to make sure they are safe.*

Elizabeth Whelan, president of the industry-funded American Council on Science and Health (ACSH), counsels that people "should remember the basic tenet of toxicology—the dose makes the poison"—a phrase used often by industry to make the point that small doses are not harmful.

The EWG report points out that science has evolved considerably since that phrase was coined in the sixteenth century. "Toxic effects don't require high doses," says EWG's Houlihan.

For instance, low doses of lead or mercury at specific stages of fetal development or infancy have been shown to cause permanent health problems.

Much of the evidence of the toxicity associated with the chemicals detected by the body burden reports comes from animal studies. And many of the same health effects turning up in the animal studies are also on the rise in the human population.

> *If somebody comes onto my land, it's trespassing, but companies can put 85 toxic substances into my body without my permission and tell me there is nothing I can do about it.*

The probability that a U.S. resident will develop some type of cancer at some point in his or her lifetime is now 1 in 2 for men, and 1 in 3 for women, according to the American Cancer Society. Many forms of cancer are on the rise in humans, including breast, prostate and testicular cancers, according to the National Cancer Institute.

Reproductive system defects and major nervous system disorders are also increasing in humans. Hypospadias, a birth defect of the penis, doubled in the United States between 1970 and 1993 and is now estimated to affect one of every 125 male babies born. Reported cases of autism are now almost 10 times higher than in the mid-1980s, according to some recent studies.

For all those diseases, there is data that either suggests or demonstrates that environmental factors may be contributing to the increase, and chemical exposures may be part of that picture, scientists say.

"There is an epidemic of breast cancer and there is an epidemic of many chronic diseases in this country and the question is, what is the contribution of this body burden that we are all bearing?" asks Michael Lerner, one of the EWG test subjects and the founder of Commonweal.

Industry counters the health worries with accusations that "chemophobics" are using the CDC study to further a political agenda.

Steven Milloy, frequent defender of the chemical industry and columnist for FoxNews.com, accused environmentalists of using the information in the CDC report to "terrorize us with yet another junk science–fueled campaign intended to advance their mindless anti-chemical agenda."

Industry defenders say that people should feel reassured by the information released by CDC. "Thanks to the CDC report, we're now more certain than ever that the synthetic chemical amounts we are routinely subjected to are trivial. We ought to feel safer than ever," said Todd Seavey of ACSH.

But industry critics question why industry has the right to contaminate people with products that may be harmful, and say industry should be held liable for chemical trespass.

"If somebody comes onto my land, it's trespassing, but companies can put 85 toxic substances into my body without my permission and tell me there is nothing I can do about it. That can't be right," says Charlotte Brody, RN, 54, director of the Washington, D.C.–based environmental group Health Care Without Harm and one of the nine subjects tested for the EWG report.

Outright Banning Works

Two encouraging findings in the CDC report point toward at least one solution to the toxic body burden in humans. The levels of cotinine (a marker for tobacco smoke) decreased in children by 58 percent, while exposure to unsafe levels of lead declined among children under age 5 from 4.4 percent to 2.2 percent—although there is debate over whether any level of lead is really safe.

The CDC also reported decreasing levels in the general population of DDT and PCBs, two substances banned in the 1970s.

"It appears that regulation, and in fact outright elimination or banning, works," says Dr. Peter Orris, director of the Occupational Health Services Institute at the University of Illinois. "These are all examples of regulatory action on the part of the government which we not only can applaud, but we now have data indicating that this works and is an effective means of social policy."

Orris says the CDC data should help set priorities for public health action.

"We need to move ahead, rapidly ahead, with mercury and other regulations," he says, including ratification of the Stockholm Treaty on Persistent Organic Pollutants (POPS). "These problems are global and not local." The United States has yet to ratify the POPS Treaty, an international agreement to ban 12 of the most harmful pollutants based on their known human health effects.

EWG recommends reform of TSCA, which the environmental group says is "so fundamentally broken that the statute needs to be rewritten." The group recommends that the chemical industry be made to disclose all internal studies about the environmental fate, human contamination and health effects of chemicals, and to thoroughly test all chemicals found in humans "for their health effects in low-dose, womb-to-tomb, multi-generational studies" focused on known target organs.

The CDC will, at least, continue to provide scientists and activists with more information about the extent of human contamination for years to come. The agency's $6.5-million biomonitoring study is "budgeted to continue at the same rate every two years into the indefinite future," says the agency's Pirkle.

The CDC plans to add new chemicals, and solicit input from other government agencies, environmental groups and industry about how to make the data more useful.

In the meantime, many activists say there is enough information available now to warrant regulations to protect people, particularly children, from industrial chemicals.

"We need to change the way of manufacturing products, shifting from protection that industry gets to protection of the consumer," says test subject Martin. She advocates for a "better safe than sorry" approach that requires manufacturers to test for safety before they are allowed to introduce chemicals into commerce.

"The fact that we are walking toxic dumps is literally the result of decisions made long ago and is not an inevitability of modern life," she says. "If there is intelligence to come up with new chemicals and come up with modern conveniences, the same intelligence exists to make it safe."

7

Environmentalists Overstate the Danger of Industrial Chemicals

Jane E. Brody

Jane E. Brody is a journalist for the New York Times *and author of several books about cooking and nutrition.*

While many Americans worry about the chemicals in the environment, their fears are overblown. Industrial toxins found in the human body may not be desirable, but there is little proof that they are harmful in small doses. In fact, Americans are healthier and living longer than at any time in history. Eliminating chemicals from the environment would be an impossible task. The benefits provided by pesticides, plastics, petroleum, and other products of America's chemical industry far outweigh possible risks.

Spared from worry about whether they will have enough to eat today or a roof over their heads tomorrow, most Americans have the luxury of worrying about the hazards that may be lurking in their air, water and food as a result of all this progress and affluence.

We are healthier, live longer, have more sources of pleasure and convenience and more regulations of industrial and agricultural production than ever, but we are also more worried about the costs to our health of environmental contaminants. This is not to say there is nothing to worry about. In an ideal world, progress would result only in benefits, no risks. In an ideal world, we would be able to produce, organically and inexpensively, all the food we need and the food our importers rely on. In an ideal world, manufacturing would leave no residues in air, water or soil, and people would be smart and disciplined enough to resist exposure to health-robbing substances like tobacco and consistent about using protective devices like seat belts, helmets end condoms.

> *// Too often, the risks people worry most about are out of proportion to the actual dangers involved. //*

But this is not and never will be an ideal world, so bad things will occasionally happen. Regulations cannot control every risk. Besides, every regulation has a price. The millions or billions spent in compliance and enforcement might be better used in ways that would save many more lives, and sometimes the cost is not worth the potential benefit. I say "potential" because in many cases, the risks involved are only hypothetical, extrapolations from studies in laboratory animals that may have little or no bearing on people.

For example, despite widespread belief and laboratory studies in rats that link pollution to breast cancer on Long Island, this month [August 2002] an $8 million federal study found no evidence that environmental contamination from pesticides and industrial chemicals was responsible.

Why People Worry

"People are scared about environmental dangers," noted Dr. Glenn Swogger Jr., a psychiatrist in Topeka, Kan. "Being scared affects their ability to think realistically and use good judgment." Underlying these fears, he believes, are uncertainty about the effects of exposures to certain substances, a tendency to overreact and seek scapegoats in stressful situations, guilt about our affluence and an unspoken wish to return to a simpler and purer world.

Experts in risk perception say people who become agitated about real or potential risks are influenced by a number of "outrage" factors. Prominent among them is control. Is the risk voluntarily assumed or imposed by others? A woman I know who eats only organically grown food enjoys rock climbing, skiing and whitewater rafting, sports far riskier than all the chemical fertilizers, pesticides and antibiotics combined. Likewise, does it make sense for smokers to worry about pollution from a nearby factory?

In short, too often, the risks people worry most about are out of proportion to the actual dangers involved.

Next is the fairness factor. Is there a benefit to the consumer, or are consumers assuming risks resulting from benefits gained only by the manufacturer? A classic example is toxic waste dumped on a community. Or, if there are some consumer benefits, are they out of proportion to the risks? One example is the use of antibiotics in animal production, a process that has led to the spread of antibiotic-resistant bacteria.

> *Animal studies rarely reveal the possible effects, or safety, of long-term exposure to the kinds of low doses people may experience.*

Is the hazard natural or caused by people? Although there was a brief flurry of concern about radon, which emanates naturally from soil and rock, perpetual and far more intense concern arises over radioactivity from mine tailings and nuclear power plants. Yet the known cost to lives from other energy sources, including solar power, gas and oil, still far exceeds that associated with nuclear power.

How new or familiar is the risk? People worry much more about possible accidents caused by new technologies than about ones they have known about all their lives. Traditional plant-breeding techniques have resulted in no protests. But the introduction of genetically modified foods has prompted some people to pay premium prices for foods said to be free of any genetic manipulation, even if it results in more wholesome products.

Is there potential for a catastrophe? Consumers have repeatedly ranked nuclear power as the No. 1 hazard among more than two dozen activities and technologies, including smoking and handguns. Many people are far more frightened of air travel, especially after a plane crash, than they are of driving, which, mile for mile, presents a far greater risk.

Risks vs. Costs

It is not possible to anticipate, regulate and control every risk. Priorities must be assigned for risk management, with time and money devoted to those hazards best established and most likely to cause the most harm.

Not every regulation is a good investment. For example, for each premature death averted, the regulation that lists petroleum refining sludge as a hazardous waste costs $27.6 million while the rule that does the same for wood preserving chemicals costs $5.7 trillion per death avoided, according to estimates from the Office of Management and Budget.

The asbestos ban, at $110.7 million per life saved, was a bargain compared with the exposure limits placed on formaldehyde, which cost an estimated $86.2 billion per death averted.

Animal tests that result in cancer caused by a suspect substance do not necessarily apply to people. Half of all chemicals that have been tested have caused cancer in one or another experimental animal, but not always in all species or strains tested or even in both sexes. Often animal strains genetically susceptible to certain cancers are chosen for these tests. When very large doses are used in animal tests, the result is often toxicity and inflammation, which itself can cause cancer even if the substance is not carcinogenic.

A cardinal rule in toxicology is "the dose makes the poison." You can eat a dozen carrots at once with no ill effect, but 400 carrots could kill you. Animal studies rarely reveal the possible effects, or safety, of long-term exposure to the kinds of low doses people may experience.

Keep in mind that we all have livers, which accrue and detoxify small amounts of hazardous substances. Another limitation of animal tests is their usual failure to detect risks that may result from interactions between two or more otherwise innocuous substances.

Remember, too, that "natural" is not necessarily safer, and just because something is manufactured does not make it a potential hazard. Nature is hardly benign. Arsenic, hemlock and, despite its current medical applications, botulism toxin are wholly natural but also deadly.

8

Storing Nuclear Waste in Yucca Mountain Would Be Extremely Dangerous

Public Citizen

Public Citizen is a national, nonprofit consumer advocacy organization founded in 1971 that works for the rights of consumers; for clean, safe, and sustainable energy sources; and for strong health and environmental protections.

When nuclear power plants, owned by private companies, generate toxic radioactive waste, American taxpayers must pay for the storage of this spent nuclear material. The federal government has decided that Yucca Mountain in Nevada is the best place to store high-level radioactive waste until it is no longer dangerous—for 240,000 years. There is no way that the storage site will remain safe for more than two thousand centuries. The canisters slated to hold the waste have already been shown to corrode rapidly and leak from the stress of the radioactive material. If they were placed in Yucca Mountain, the leaking waste would mix with rainwater that runs into the storage area at the present time. This combination will ensure that the groundwater beneath the site will be contaminated with radioactive waste within the foreseeable future. Yucca Mountain is also in an active earthquake zone. A strong earthquake could break the storage containers and allow nuclear waste to leak. Therefore, the idea of

storing radioactive waste at Yucca Mountain is a deadly
government boondoggle.

H igh-level radioactive waste is produced at commercial nuclear power plants and at nuclear materials production defense facilities. Nuclear fuel is made of solid pellets of enriched
uranium. The pellets are sealed in tubes, which are bundled together to form a nuclear fuel assembly. The assemblies are put
inside a nuclear reactor and used to generate heat to make electricity. The fuel will be used until it is spent or no longer effi-
cient in generating heat. Once a year, approximately one-third
of the nuclear fuel inside a reactor is removed and replaced by
new fuel assemblies. The used, irradiated fuel—sometimes
called "spent fuel"—is highly radioactive and is the primary
form of high-level nuclear waste.

When irradiated fuel is removed from a reactor, it is extremely hot, so all nuclear power plants have "spent fuel
pools," where the waste is placed in order to cool and allow
some of the radioactivity to decay. Each reactor is allotted only
a certain amount of pool space, and when the pools are full,
the reactors either must shut down or move some of their older
waste to above ground concrete or steel containers called dry
casks. When the irradiated fuel is moved into dry cask storage,
it is still highly radioactive.

Storage Is Expensive

Past claims that nuclear energy would be "too cheap to meter"
have proven false. Storage of nuclear waste is very expensive.
Rather than requiring the nuclear industry to be fully liable for
the costs of long-term management of the waste it generates,
the government has assumed this responsibility. Nuclear power
plants add fees to their ratepayers' bills for the Nuclear Waste
Fund, established by the federal government in 1982 to research ways to dispose of nuclear waste. The money in this
fund, supplemented by defense appropriations, is being used to
pay for the Yucca Mountain Project.

Yucca Mountain, located approximately 80 miles north-
west of Las Vegas, Nevada, is the only site in the U.S. being considered for a high-level nuclear waste repository. The proposed
repository would contain 70,000 metric tons (77,000 U.S. standard tons) of nuclear waste, including 63,000 metric tons of
"spent fuel" from commercial nuclear power plants and 7,000

metric tons of high-level waste from the U.S. Department of Energy (DOE) weapons complex. High-level radioactive waste is currently in storage at 77 sites in the U.S. Commercial nuclear power plants have generated about 45,000 metric tons of "spent fuel" to date and this amount is expected to at least double by 2035. In addition, U.S. weapons and research activities have produced more than 2,500 metric tons of "spent fuel" and approximately 100 million gallons of liquid high-level waste. Because a Yucca Mountain repository could not accommodate all the waste (its capacity would be capped at 70,000 tons), it is inaccurate to characterize the project as a proposal for nuclear waste consolidation. Moreover, since irradiated fuel must decay in a "cooling pool" for at least five years before it can be transported, at least five years' worth of nuclear waste (100–150 metric tons) would remain at each operating reactor even if the proposed repository opens. . . .

> *It now seems to be a question of when—not if—the waste from a Yucca Mountain repository would contaminate the surrounding environment.*

If all goes according to the DOE's plan, waste will be accepted at Yucca Mountain beginning in 2010 and will continue to arrive at Yucca Mountain for at least 24 years, with the final "emplacement" activities ending after 2035. However, delays are likely according to the General Accounting Office (GAO), the investigative arm of Congress. In May 2002, the GAO testified that "DOE currently does not have a reliable estimate of when, and at what cost, a license application can be submitted or a repository can be opened. . ."

Problems with the Yucca Mountain Site

Groundwater Contamination

The DOE talks about "disposing of" nuclear waste. But nuclear waste cannot be disposed of; it only can be stored. When stored, there is always the danger that radiation will escape. The original concept of a geologic repository was for a site with "natural barriers" sufficient to contain nuclear waste throughout the 240,000 years that it remains dangerously radioactive. But the DOE is finding more and more problems with the natural barrier system at Yucca Mountain, and the agency appears to be scrambling to piece together an engineered barrier system instead. DOE's repository design proposals have been criticized by the Nuclear Waste Technical Review Board for the high and unquantified levels of uncertainty involved in . . . engineered barriers (i.e., waste storage canisters). Indeed, it now seems to be a question of when—not if—the waste from a Yucca Mountain repository would contaminate the surrounding environment.

A freshwater aquifer lies beneath Yucca Mountain. If radioactive waste from a repository leaks, it would jeopardize the health of nearby residents, who depend on that aquifer as their sole source of drinking water. The National Academy of Sciences has identified the groundwater pathway as a significant pathway of exposure in the vicinity of the Yucca Mountain site. . . .

Earthquakes

Nevada ranks third in the nation for current seismic activity. Since 1976, there have been more than 600 seismic events of a magnitude greater than 2.5 within a 50-mile radius of Yucca Mountain. Native Americans in the area call Yucca Mountain a rolling hill and speak of its constant movement. In 1992, an earthquake with a magnitude of 5.6 occurred that caused damage to a DOE field office building in the area. As recently as June 14, 2002, an earthquake measuring 4.4 on the Richter scale was recorded just 12 miles from Yucca Mountain.

Should a strong earthquake hit the Yucca Mountain area while nuclear waste is stored there, disastrous consequences could result. The storage canisters could break open and portions of the mountain could collapse, restricting access to the broken canisters inside. Some scientists also believe that a significant rise in groundwater levels could occur as the result of an earthquake, possibly flooding the repository. This type of event would surely compromise the integrity of the nuclear waste containers and contaminate the groundwater beneath Yucca Mountain.

Transporting High-Level Radioactive Waste

If the Yucca Mountain repository proposal is approved and licensed, waste will be transported to Nevada from the 77 sites where it is currently stored. The DOE has not indicated whether it will transport the nuclear waste by truck or by train, but either way, the transportation will take at least 24 years and involve tens of thousands of shipments. The most recent analysis indicates that this deadly cargo would pass through 44 states and the District of Columbia en route to Yucca Mountain.

Although the DOE has refused to finalize the transportation routes it would use to haul this extremely hazardous material across the country, Department of Transportation regulations strictly limit the potential routes. . . .

Whether the waste is transported by truck or rail, it will be carried in transportation casks. . . . Current NRC [Nuclear Regulatory Commission] regulations allow these casks to emit radiation equivalent to a chest x-ray . . . at 6.5 feet from the cask surface.

These casks have never been fully tested. In 1987, the NRC sponsored a study, commonly referred to as the "Modal Study," by the Lawrence Livermore National Laboratories, that used computer modeling to predict cask responses to accident conditions. The study was inadequate in that it did not include full-scale physical testing of the casks, and the conditions that were used in the computer analysis did not represent real-life scenarios. The NRC has contracted with Sandia National Labs to conduct another study (the "Package Performance Study"), but this new study will not be completed until 2005.

> *Should a strong earthquake hit the Yucca Mountain area while nuclear waste is stored there, disastrous consequences could result.*

Transporting nuclear waste poses inherent dangers, particularly in the event of an accident (e.g., if an equipment failure or human error causes the waste to roll off the truck or leak) or crash. It is unclear whether hospitals, police and rescue personnel along transportation routes would have the capacity to respond effectively to a nuclear waste emergency.

State of Nevada analysis indicates that 161 accidents could be expected involving Yucca Mountain shipments under a "mostly truck" shipping scenario, or 390 under a "mostly train" scenario. As part of the 1986 Environmental Assessment for the Yucca Mountain repository site, the DOE conducted a study that found that a severe accident in a rural area involving a high-speed impact, lengthy fire and fuel oxidation would contaminate a 42-square-mile area, require 462 days to clean up and cost $620 million. The health, economic and environmental impacts of such an accident could devastate a community.

Transporting high-level nuclear waste to Yucca Mountain could cause other problems for communities en route. The potential for terrorist attacks on waste shipments has not been satisfactorily addressed in DOE's Yucca Mountain proposals. Also, property values have been shown to decline along nuclear waste transportation routes even without an accident or act of sabotage.

> *A severe accident in a rural area involving a high-speed impact . . . would contaminate a 42-square-mile area, require 462 days to clean up and cost $620 million.*

Although the Yucca Mountain Project would launch an unprecedented nuclear transportation scheme, the DOE's repository proposal inadequately addresses transportation issues. Yet, logically, the safety and viability of getting the waste to Nevada is an intrinsic aspect of considerations surrounding the repository proposal. It would therefore be premature at best for Congress to accept a Yucca Mountain site recommendation from DOE with so many questions relating to transportation unanswered.

Flawed Process

The dramatically flawed process that has characterized the repository project undermines the credibility of the DOE's site characterization and site recommendation activities at Yucca Mountain. Radiation protection standards (set by the EPA [Environmental Protection Agency]) and repository siting guidelines (set by the DOE) were rewritten to avoid disqualifying the Yucca Mountain site, sacrificing public health and safety to nuclear industry interests.

According to analysis by Public Citizen's Congress Watch, Energy Secretary Spencer Abraham accepted $82,728 from the nuclear industry during the last election cycle (1995 through Sept. 30, 2000). A . . . request [by environmental group Public Citizen] that Abraham recuse himself from Yucca Mountain dealings because of this apparent conflict of interest was rejected.

In November 2001, a DOE Inspector General investigation uncovered other apparent conflicts of interest involving contractors on the Yucca Mountain Project. According to the report, the law firm Winston & Strawn was simultaneously employed as counsel to the DOE, working on the Yucca Mountain Project, and registered as a member of and lobbyist for the Nuclear Energy Institute, the pro-repository nuclear industry trade group, between 1992 and 2001. Although Winston & Strawn resigned from the Yucca Mountain Project in the wake of this scandal, the firm's work was not withdrawn. A thorough review is urgently needed of the causes and consequences of DOE contractor conflict of interest and the apparent pro-industry bias in the agency's site characterization and site recommendation activities.

Sound science has also been compromised in the Yucca Mountain Project. A report issued last December [2002] by the General Accounting Office concluded that the DOE lacks the research and data to substantiate its repository proposal. Similarly, in a letter dated January 24, 2002, the presidentially appointed Nuclear Waste Technical Review Board advised Congress that "the technical basis for the DOE's repository performance estimates is weak to moderate."

Public Citizen advocates isolating high-level radioactive waste as close as safely possible to the reactor where it was generated until a satisfactory national solution to the nuclear waste problem is found.

9

Yucca Mountain Is the Best Place to Store Nuclear Waste

U.S. Department of Energy

The U.S. Department of Energy's mission is to protect national security by ensuring a safe and reliable energy supply. It is also responsible for disposing of the nation's radioactive waste.

The American government and industry sources have been generating high-level nuclear waste since the 1940s. This radioactive matter has been accumulating at more than 130 sites around the country. This is a dangerous situation since most of the facilities where the materials are located are not designed for long-term storage. The storage casks can leak waste that is deadly to humans and destructive to the environment. The facilities are also vulnerable to terrorist attack. To alleviate this problem, Congress passed the Nuclear Waste Policy Act in 1987, directing the secretary of energy to analyze the feasibility of storing nuclear waste at Yucca Mountain in Nevada. Since that time, the most talented scientists and engineers in the nation have participated in designing and building the Yucca site. Yucca Mountain is the safest place in the United States for long-term storage of radioactive waste. Government and industry owe it to this and future generations to carefully transport nuclear waste to Yucca Mountain, where it will be safely stored for thousand of years.

U.S. Department of Energy, Office of Civilian Radioactive Waste Management, "Why Yucca Mountain?" www.ocrwm.doe.gov, 2002.

The U.S. Navy's nuclear-powered vessels, the nation's past production and ongoing dismantlement of nuclear weapons, the commercial generation of 20 percent of our country's electricity, and many research and development activities produce high-level radioactive waste. These radioactive materials have accumulated since the mid-1940s and are currently stored in temporary facilities at some 131 sites in 39 states.

> *Commercial spent nuclear fuel is currently stored in cooling pools or dry casks designed for relatively short lifespans.*

Commercial spent nuclear fuel is currently stored in cooling pools or dry casks designed for relatively short lifespans. Most of these temporary storage sites are near large population centers, and because nuclear reactors require abundant water, they are also near rivers, lakes, and seacoasts. If not maintained and safeguarded, this material could seep into groundwater and travel in storm and snowmelt runoff into the nearby bodies of water. Should this occur, all U.S. coastlines could suffer negative consequences, affecting millions of Americans. Moreover, at least 20 major waterways currently supplying household water for more than 30 million Americans could be impacted. In all, more than 161 million Americans reside within 75 miles of where spent nuclear fuel and high-level radioactive waste are stored, closer than the residents of Las Vegas are to Yucca Mountain.

Congress Created a Legal Obligation

In 1982 Congress acted to establish a comprehensive federal policy to resolve the national problem of what to do with wastes from nuclear reactors and defense facilities. The policy centers on deep geologic disposal of high-level radioactive waste.

In passing the Nuclear Waste Policy Act, Congress assigned the primary responsibility for implementing this national policy to the Department of Energy [DOE]. Congress also identified specific actions to be undertaken by the Secretary of Energy in characterizing a site and deciding whether to recommend approval of the site to the President. In 1987, Congress directed that only Yucca Mountain be characterized for potential use as a repository. The United States is following the open, orderly, and legally specified process of the Nuclear Waste Policy Act toward a decision on whether Yucca Mountain is a suitable site for a repository and, if so, whether to apply for authorization to construct.

There is a worldwide consensus that deep geologic disposal, the approach being followed by the United States, is the only scientifically credible, long-term solution for managing high-level radioactive waste. For more than 20 years, many of our nation's top scientists and engineers have studied Yucca Mountain in Nevada to determine if this arid site would be a suitable location for development of the nation's first repository for the geologic disposal of high-level radioactive waste. They have concluded that a repository at Yucca Mountain would protect public health and safety; preserve the quality of the environment; allow the environmental cleanup of Cold War weapons facilities; protect the nation from acts of terrorism; and support a sound energy policy.

Allowing the Environmental Cleanup of Cold War Weapons Facilities

The production of nuclear weapons during World War II and the Cold War resulted in a legacy of high-level radioactive waste and spent nuclear fuel that is currently stored in Washington, South Carolina, and Idaho. Large volumes of high-level radioactive waste were created in the past when spent nuclear fuel was reprocessed to extract plutonium for weapons use. The high-level waste left over from that process exists in liquid and solid forms. Federal sites where this liquid waste has been stored, and in some instances has leaked from holding tanks, require varying degrees of remediation. The cleanup and decommissioning of the former weapons-production sites will require permanent disposal of all these materials, including solidified liquid waste.

Safeguard from Terrorism

Deep geologic disposal will safeguard radioactive waste from deliberate acts of sabotage or terrorism. No reasonably conceivable attack at the surface of a repository could have a significant impact on the high-level waste contained in robust metal containers some 1,000 feet underground. In addition, the Yucca Mountain site is remotely located on federal land, with restricted access, and adjacent to the Nevada Test Site. At the Nevada Test Site the United States has conducted over 800 nuclear weapon tests. The test site has a highly trained and effective rapid-response security force and is surrounded on three sides by the Nellis Air Force Range, all with restricted air space.

> *Nuclear materials would be secure in a closed and sealed geologic repository where unauthorized removal would be virtually impossible.*

Many of our nation's large naval vessels are powered by nuclear reactors that generate a small but strategic amount of spent nuclear fuel. The waste from naval operations is currently being stored at the Idaho National Environmental and Engineering Laboratory while awaiting final disposal. This waste must be disposed of in order to maintain our naval vigilance, now and in the future.

The United States has provided fuel for use in research reactors in both U.S. and foreign universities and laboratories. To support nuclear non-proliferation objectives, these laboratories are required to return the spent fuel. These domestic and foreign spent fuels are being stored at Savannah River, South Carolina, and at the Idaho National Engineering and Environmental Laboratory while awaiting disposal in a repository.

The end of the Cold War has brought the welcome challenge of disposing of approximately 50 metric tons of surplus weapons-usable plutonium. Nuclear materials would be secure in a closed and sealed geologic repository where unauthorized removal would be virtually impossible. By permanently disposing of its own surplus nuclear materials, the United States would encourage other nations to do the same.

Supporting a Sound Energy Policy

Preserving the capabilities to generate electric power using nuclear energy is important to a balanced energy policy. Not only does nuclear power decrease our dependence on foreign oil, but it also keeps the price of other energy alternatives low. The preservation of energy options will not be possible without permanent disposal of the spent nuclear fuel.

As utilities have moved more and more spent fuel out of crowded cooling pools into outside, aboveground storage casks, the amounts of spent fuel stored onsite are rapidly approaching limits agreed upon between utilities and state governing bodies. When these limits are reached, new or additional storage will have to be renegotiated. In some cases, the reactors may have no option but to close down prematurely, and consumers will have to pay the increased costs of replacement power. Moreover, the costs for additional onsite dry storage have been rising rapidly.

How Do We Know It Is Safe?

The natural barriers work in concert with additional man-made barriers to isolate waste from the accessible environment for tens of thousands of years. Scientists have identified five key attributes that are important to long-term performance within the Yucca Mountain disposal system:

Limited water entering emplacement tunnels

The climate at Yucca Mountain is arid, with precipitation averaging about 7.5 inches per year. Future climates during the regulatory compliance period are expected to be slightly cooler and produce a mean annual precipitation of about 12.5 inches. Little of this precipitation percolates into the mountain; nearly all of it (about 95 percent) either runs off, is picked up by the root systems of vegetation, or is lost to evaporation. This significantly limits the amount of water available to infiltrate the surface, move down through the thousand feet of unsaturated rock, and seep into emplacement tunnels.

Yucca Mountain consists of alternating layers of welded and nonwelded volcanic tuff: welded tuff at the surface, welded tuff at the level of the repository, and layers of nonwelded tuffs above and below the level of the repository. These nonwelded units contain few fractures; thus, they delay the downward flow of moisture into the welded tuff layer below, where the repository would be located. At the repository level, water in small fractures has a tendency to remain in the fractures rather than flow into larger openings, such as tunnels.

Long-lived waste package and drip shield

The DOE has designed a titanium drip shield and a waste container to work in concert with the natural barriers in the mountain. The drip shield and Alloy 22 outer barrier of the waste package would be expected to have long lifetimes in the repository environment. Alloy 22, the outer barrier material of the waste package, is very corrosion-resistant, with general corrosion expected to penetrate only about 0.03 inches of this outer layer of material in 10,000 years. The Titanium Grade 7 is also corrosion-resistant, with general corrosion expected to penetrate only about 0.08 inches, of the 0.6 inches, in 10,000 years. Only about 1 percent of the waste packages are projected to lose their integrity during the first 80,000 years.

Limited release of radionuclides from the engineered barriers

Even though the waste packages and drip shields are expected to be long-lived in the repository environment, the advanced computer simulations predict some eventual loss of waste package integrity. Even if water were to penetrate a waste package, several characteristics of the waste forms and the natural character of the repository rocks and water would limit radionuclide releases. In the early periods after closure, because of the warm temperatures, much of the water that penetrates the waste package will evaporate. The solid waste forms will not dissolve rapidly in the water expected in the repository environment. In addition, crushed tuff, which would be placed under the waste package and support pallet, would also delay the movement of radionuclides.

Delay and dilution of radionuclide concentrations by the natural barriers

Eventually, the engineered barrier systems could suffer some loss of integrity, and small amounts of water could contact waste, dissolve it, and carry some radionuclides out of the repository and into the rock below. The repository level is in the unsaturated zone, where the microscopic holes in the rock are only partially filled with water. The water table lies, on average, 1,000 feet below the repository level. At the proposed repository level, the host rock is fractured, and these fractures provide the main pathways for water and radionuclide transport through this zone. As water flows through fractures, dissolved radionuclides would diffuse into and out of the pores in the rock, increasing both the time it takes for radionuclides to move from the repository and the likelihood that they will be exposed to sorbing minerals (minerals that attract and hold them).

Rock units in both the unsaturated zone and the saturated zone at Yucca Mountain contain minerals called zeolites that work like activated charcoal to absorb and delay many radionuclides. The degree of delay introduced by the saturated zone differs greatly for various radionuclides, depending on their capacity to sorb onto mineral surfaces and colloids (very small particles of clay or other material). Strongly sorbing radionuclide species have transport times that range from tens of thousands to millions of years, and do not significantly contribute to calculated doses during the 10,000-year period of regulatory compliance. In contrast, nonsorbing and weakly sorbing radionuclides have the potential to be carried to the accessible environment by groundwater thousands of years in the future—when the waste package and the waste forms have lost their integrity.

> *By 2040 this nation could generate almost 108,000 metric tons of spent nuclear fuel and more than 22,000 canisters of high-level radioactive waste.*

Flow paths from beneath the repository are generally southerly toward the Amargosa Desert. Radionuclide migration through the saturated zone results in dilution and reduced radionuclide concentrations in groundwater. Additionally, the water in the Amargosa Desert is in an isolated hydrologic basin that does not connect to any lakes or rivers that discharge into the ocean.

Conditions at Yucca Mountain

Yucca Mountain provides an environment in which hydrogeologic conditions important to waste isolation (e.g., a thick unsaturated zone with low rates of water movement) have changed little, if at all, for millions of years. The DOE considered three specific disruptive processes and events (i.e., volcanism, ground motion from seismic events, and nuclear [accidents that could release high levels of radiation]) that could impact the performance of a repository at Yucca Mountain.

Of the three, volcanism resulted in a low but calculable dose during the regulatory period. The likelihood of the repository being disrupted by a volcano is extremely small (about 1 chance in 70 million per year) and the estimated probability weighted dose would be less than one percent of the NRC [Nuclear Regulatory Commission] and EPA [Environmental Protection Agency] radiation protection standards. The NRC requires all nuclear facilities to withstand expected natural phenomena like earthquakes. Criticality was found to have such a low likelihood that it is not necessary to consider further according to regulations.

Doing Nothing Is Not an Option

The United States currently has about 47,500 metric tons of spent nuclear fuel (45,000 from commercial power reactors and 2,500 from defense reactors). In addition, DOE is currently processing over 100 million gallons of liquid high-level radioactive waste from defense activities and stabilizing it into borosilicate glass. By 2040 this nation could generate almost 108,000 metric tons of spent nuclear fuel and more than 22,000 canisters of high-level radioactive waste glass. This waste must be properly managed to prevent adverse impacts to the health and safety of millions of Americans and to the environment.

In the aftermath of the tragic events of September 11 [2001], the DOE, along with other federal agencies, is continuing to assess measures that could be taken to minimize the risk or consequences of radiological sabotage or terrorist attacks against our nation's nuclear facilities and spent nuclear fuel shipments. Deep geologic disposal of spent nuclear fuel and high-level radioactive waste provides optimal security by emplacing the material so far underground that it would provide protection from both inadvertent and intentional human intrusion, including potential terrorist activities.

Our Obligation to Future Generations

The Nuclear Waste Policy Act requires that the generators and owners of the high-level radioactive waste be responsible for disposing of such waste. This requirement derives from the conviction that the generations receiving the benefits of nuclear power are also responsible for the disposal of the waste. It is widely believed that future generations should not bear these burdens when the means for safe disposal are available to this generation.

We as a nation must also preserve the flexibility for future generations to make the final decisions on whether to close the repository or retrieve the waste to reclaim its energy value or take advantage of future technology.

10

Terrorists Can Turn Nuclear Waste into Deadly "Dirty Bombs"

Harbhajan Singh Sandhu

Harbhajan Singh Sandhu is a nuclear physicist, professor emeritus of physics and astronomy at California State University, Northridge, and author of the novel Wayward Brahmin.

Nuclear power plants in the United States generate over one ton of radioactive waste annually. This deadly material, which will remain extremely hazardous for thousands of years, is stored outdoors at nuclear reactor sites across the nation. In the coming years, the government plans to transport this toxic cargo on trucks and trains to a permanent repository in Nevada. Whether it is stored or moved, determined terrorists could steal some of this nuclear waste with relative ease and use it to build "dirty bombs" that use common explosive devices to spread deadly radioactive waste. If such a device were to be detonated in a major city, it would kill or injure thousands, cause trillions of dollars in property damage, and create massive panic among the general public. The nuclear power industry needs to secure this waste and rethink plans to move it, or Americans might suffer the consequences.

Nuclear waste is one of the most potent weapons that could be used by terrorists in so-called "dirty bombs" (radioactive material spread by a common explosive). Especially, if it is laced with the type of high-level radioactive spent-fuel pro-

68

duced by irradiated uranium that commercial nuclear power plants generate daily. This is one of the most dangerous of radioactive wastes. Although it comprises less than one per cent of the total radioactive waste in the U.S., it accounts for ninety-five per cent of all radioactivity generated. A single commercial nuclear reactor typically discharges about thirty tons of irradiated fuel annually. Currently an estimated 77,000 tons of radioactive waste lies in cooling pools at over 100 commercial nuclear reactors awaiting transport to a permanent nuclear waste storage facility. Such a repository is expected to open in the year 2010 in Nevada at Yucca Mountain. Until then, these reactors will continue to add about 2000 tons of new spent-fuel waste annually to our nation's existing inventory.

A Fool's Game

Setting aside the highly improbable scenarios of terrorists actually acquiring an existing nuclear bomb or even constructing one—which would require a substantial amount of weapons-grade plutonium, a sophisticated design and trigger mechanism—accessing such high-level nuclear waste for use in "dirty bombs" represents a viable terrorists' alternative. Herein lies the heart of our dilemma, as it constitutes a critical public danger in our post 9-11 era, one that is next only to an actual nuclear bomb detonation. Here is why. . . .

> *Plutonium-239 is one of the most lethally toxic isotopes; one pound of it, if evenly spread over a large metropolitan area, could cause an estimated one million cancer related deaths.*

The main body of power reactors is generally placed in a reinforced containment building able to withstand a significant impact or collision. However, a huge amount of nuclear waste is stored at the reactor site outside the containment building in cooling pools and in stacks of space-saving fabricated columns. Typically, this waste can contain a blend of varying levels of hundreds of radioisotopes with different half-lives (a half-life is the amount of time it takes to reduce the level of radioactivity to one half that of the original). A radioisotope is considered to be highly dangerous for about ten half-lives. This means that plutonium-239, with half-life of 24,400 years, is dangerous for a quarter of a million years. Plutonium-239 is one of the most lethally toxic isotopes; one pound of it, if evenly spread over a large metropolitan area, could cause an estimated one million cancer related deaths. Many other isotopes in radioactive sludge such as iodine-129, neptunium-237, cesium-137, uranium-238, and zirconium-93, have half-lives in the millions of years. From a terrorist's perspective, this nuclear waste represents a veritable gold mine for future "dirty bomb" production. Indeed, it is the Mother Lode of Mother Lodes with 77,000 tons of it already lying around and an estimated 2,000 tons being produced annually—in the United States alone. Beyond that, our government openly admits that the radioactive waste stored around the country cannot be adequately protected against terrorists' attacks. Hence its reason for planning to ship this deadly nuclear waste to Yucca Mountain along our public transport systems. This is a fool's game that terrorists can take advantage of.

Thousands of Moving Targets

Besides the much publicized psychological panic caused by a "dirty bomb" laced with even low-level radioactivity, the detonation of one using high-level nuclear waste, like plutonium-239, into the atmosphere would constitute an irreversible environmental tragedy; one with deadly long-term public health consequences.

> *Our government openly admits that the radioactive waste stored around the country cannot be adequately protected against terrorists' attacks.*

This scenario is further aggravated by the need to transport huge amounts of high-level waste from the hundreds of temporary cooling pools around the nation to processing facilities, and finally to Yucca Mountain for "permanent" storage. To ship the existing inventory of nuclear waste to this site will require an estimated 108,500 shipments over a period of thirty-eight years. The Department of Energy (DOE) plans to transport this deadly waste in specially engineered containers. Now, although these transport containers were developed to move "vitrified" nuclear waste (waste that has been solidified in a matrix of borosilicate [hardened] glass) by truck or train, researchers have only tested them using computer simulations—no real world testing has been undertaken. Nevertheless, it is expected that these containers will withstand the high impact of a train or truck collision. Unfortunately, they are also capable of being pierced or shattered by a rocket bomb or a suicide detonation—common tools of terrorist trade. These shipments of deadly nuclear waste—all 108,500 of them over thirty-eight years—create tens of thousands of viable moving targets for terrorists.

Whether dispersed by a "dirty bomb" or by sabotaging a transport vessel, the tens of thousands of tons of high-level nuclear waste lying around our more than [one] hundred nuclear sites, and an unspecified number of military weapon facilities, collectively constitutes a highly vulnerable terrorist target. Resolving this dilemma must be a national priority. Nuclear plants, their onsite radioactive waste security, and the current plan to transport this deadly material along our public transport corridors must be thoroughly re-examined to find rational alternatives.

11

Recycling Plutonium to Create Nuclear Reactor Fuel Is a Dangerous Idea

Lynn Hamilton

Reporter Lynn Hamilton is a contributor to AlterNet.org and the publisher of the Tybee News, *a paper for residents of Tybee Island, Georgia.*

The U.S. government has generated tons of highly toxic plutonium while building thousands of nuclear bombs over the past sixty years. Since the end of the Cold War in 1991, the Department of Defense has been decommissioning some of the nuclear weapons but has been left with the problem of what to do with the plutonium. This material is so deadly that the amount the size of a pinhead will instantly kill a person—and it will remain poisonous for 240,000 years. With the responsibility to deal with this deadly cargo, the Department of Energy has proposed recycling this weapons-grade material into mixed oxide or MOX fuel for use in nuclear power plants. This solution is as misguided as it is dangerous. The material would have to be transported from storage sites to the Savannah River processing plant in South Carolina, leaving trucks exposed to terrorists. If some of the plutonium fell into the wrong hands, it could be used to launch a catastrophic terrorist attack that could kill untold numbers of Americans and cost billions of dollars. In addition, the reprocessing method poses an extreme threat to the environment and to human lives. The government should bury plutonium waste deep in the ground and forget about recycling it.

The spy has come in from the cold, and Russia has agreed to lay down its nuclear weapons alongside the US. But one leftover from the cold war—surplus weapons plutonium—is, in some minds, a possible threat in the hands of our new enemies—Middle Eastern terrorists.

The Department of Energy (DOE) has a novel idea: to "recycle" that plutonium into energy with which we can heat and light our homes and run our businesses. Plutonium can be purified and combined with a greater quantity of uranium oxide to produce mixed oxide fuel, known as MOX, which can, in turn, be used as nuclear reactor fuel. The DOE has signed a contract with a nuclear conglomerate, Duke COGEMA Stone and Webster, to produce MOX at the Savannah River Site (SRS) outside Augusta, South Carolina. Production is scheduled to begin in 2007, and, in the meantime, the project is up for public comment.

Will MOX production neutralize our weapons grade plutonium, making this a safer world, or will transporting plutonium to South Carolina and manufacturing MOX pose a danger to southeastern communities and a possible invitation to terrorists?

> *Scientists have wondered if producing MOX might not present a clear and present danger.*

Duke COGEMA Stone and Webster say that MOX can be safely produced and transported, but environmentalists and others who oppose nuclear power and weapons have heated objections to the MOX program which has yet to be licensed by the Nuclear Regulatory Commission (NRC). MOX opponents say there's a safer way to neutralize the threat posed by leftover plutonium. It could be immobilized in canisters and stored in the Yucca Mountains. To do otherwise perpetuates the dangerous use of nuclear energy and even leads to future bomb production, some say. The DOE developed a detailed program for immobilizing at least some of our surplus weapons plutonium, then further angered environmentalists by declaring, at the beginning of this year [2002], that all of it would be turned over for MOX production instead.

"Just spend the money and immobilize this stuff," said

[antinuclear activist] Jody Lanier at a recent NRC-hosted meeting in Savannah, Georgia, 90 miles southeast of the Savannah River Site. . . .

"Where will we go if there's a terrorist attack?" asked Lanier. "They're trying to shove a giant poo poo platter down our throat."

Truckin' Plutonium

The transportation of plutonium to and from the Savannah River Site has been a colorful issue since [June 2002 when] South Carolina Governor Jim Hodges vowed to lie in the road, if necessary, to keep plutonium shipments out of his state.

The plutonium will make four trips altogether. First, the raw surplus material will be trucked in to the Savannah River Site. Most of it will probably come from weapons production sites in Colorado and Texas, according to Sara Barczak who represents Georgians for Clean Energy. When it has been converted to MOX, the fuel will then be transported to two nuclear stations in the southeast where it will serve as fuel.

After that, according to Barczak, the spent fuel by-product has to go back to the Savannah River Site before it makes its final journey to a "geologic repository" where it will remain in, hopefully, accident-proof canisters.

Duke COGEMA Stone and Webster have distributed a reassuringly detailed fact sheet about phase two of the transportation process: the transport of MOX fuel to the nuclear reactors. MOX packages are designed to sustain fire, cold, water immersion and a 30-foot drop, and they will be transported in tractor-trailers under armed guard.

> *Producing MOX is not a simple case of 'waste not, want not.' MOX production generates a tremendous amount of waste at several stages.*

But it's the first phase of the journey—the transport of unprocessed weapons plutonium to the Savannah River Site in the first place—that's of more concern to Barczak. "The plutonium oxide at Rocky Flats [the weapons production facility in Colorado] is highly dispersible in air," says Barczak. "It's the good stuff. From a terrorist perspective, you've got the form that they want on the roadways."

When asked about the transport of plutonium to the Savannah River Site, Duke COGEMA Stone and Webster Communications Coordinator Todd Kaish said the DOE would be handling all the transportation for this project.

Getting information from the Department of Energy can be a challenge. The department website lists a "nuclear safety hotline" which you might think would directly address the issue. Upon dialing it, however, you get a recorded advertisement for "the talk line" which promises "exciting people nationwide" in a breathy, excited voice.

A Nuclear Experiment

Is the MOX program a safe, well-researched enterprise or an experiment being foisted on the southeastern United States which have been slow to stick up for their rights to clean air and water?

Making MOX out of warhead plutonium was first proposed by the National Academy of Sciences in 1994. The academy wrote that to reduce the "clear and present danger" posed by leftover bomb plutonium, it should be rendered as harmless as plutonium that's been run through a reactor and turned into energy. The "spent fuel standard," the academy called it. Since then, however, other scientists have wondered if producing MOX might not present a clear and present danger in and of itself.

> // *The additional risks posed by MOX fuel compared to uranium fuel are even greater than previously assumed.* //

Duke COGEMA Stone and Webster say they can safely produce the new fuel in a facility which will be modeled on MOX-producing plants in France. COGEMA, one of the partners in the enterprise, is the French firm that, along with Belgonucleaire, already operates three industrial MOX plants in France and Belgium where the majority of the world's MOX fuel is produced.

Duke COGEMA Stone and Webster represent the production of MOX as something that is already being routinely done in France and Belgium—and at a much bigger scale than that proposed in the US. MOX plants in France and Belgium produce fuel for 30 nuclear units in contrast to the modest two proposed by America's DOE.

But MOX opponents say that's a misleading representation. France and Belgium are, indeed, producing MOX, but not from the weapons-grade plutonium that's slated for use at the SRS. The American project is experimental, says Barczak.

"They [the French] make it from commercial plutonium," she explains. "Every nuclear power plant creates plutonium, so they take those spent fuel rods and reprocess them and extract the plutonium and make it into MOX. The difference is the commercial grade is different from the weapons-grade plutonium. It's not the same thing. It's new," says Barczak.

Before it can become a MOX ingredient, all plutonium—both commercial and weapons-grade—has to be purified. Weapons plutonium, however, contains a troublesome chemical called gallium, according to Arjun Markhijani and Anita Seth of the Institute for Energy and Environmental Research.

"Gallium complicates the MOX fuel fabrication process and therefore it must be almost completely removed from weapons grade plutonium prior to fuel fabrication," they write in an essay titled "The Use of Weapons Plutonium as Reactor Fuel."

Can You Call It Recycling?

A program which reshapes a dangerous white elephant into something we all need—energy—is bound to look attractive to many Americans. Our frontier heritage cries out to be inventive with resources and not to waste anything that has some residual value.

But producing MOX is not a simple case of "waste not, want not." MOX production generates a tremendous amount of waste at several stages, according to MOX fabrication opponents.

Purifying plutonium, alone, "involves huge liquid waste discharges," Markhijani and Seth write. They refer to a process called "aqueous polishing" which is currently used to purify commercial plutonium. Plutonium could be purified using a dry process, which, Markhijani and Seth imply, would be cleaner, but "dry processes . . . have not yet been developed beyond the laboratory scale." Such a process could be developed in five years, Markhijani and Seth write, which would make it available in time for MOX production, currently scheduled to begin in 2007. But Duke COGEMA Stone and Webster have no intention of using a dry process, according to Communications Coordinator Todd Kaish.

"The aqueous polishing process is the process that we will be using at the MOX facility," says Kaish.

So making MOX will involve much chemical waste. And, because producing nuclear energy always involves radioactive waste, MOX will create some more waste at the reactor end, when it is converted into electricity.

The resulting spent fuel "will be stored in a geologic repository," according to Duke COGEMA Stone and Webster. In other words, surplus plutonium ends up in storage in the Yucca Mountains one way or another. It could be immobilized and go straight there without making any detours, or, as is proposed by DOE, it can generate tons of waste along the way.

Someone Else's Backyard

MOX is scheduled for production at the notorious Savannah River Site, called a Superfund site by clean energy activists.

"It is the site that has the most radioactivity of any DOE site in the country," Barczak says. "And it has the second largest volume."

At the scoping meeting in Savannah, Lanier said the MOX program would only add to "the overburdened waste stream that's already at Savannah River Site."

"We've got all this other waste from over 50 years in leaky tanks," said Lanier, who voiced his concern that contamination from SRS could encroach on the Floridian aquifer, the region's principle source of drinking water.

Lanier was far from alone in this opinion. Green Party leader William Pleasant said the SRS has "been run sloppily for 50 years." Fred Nadelman of Citizens for Clean Air and Water said SRS should be "cleaned up, shut down, and turned into a park." Georgia State Representative Regina Thomas said that the SRS is the site of too much contamination already.

In fact, the tone of citizen input at the Savannah meeting—90 miles downstream and downwind of the SRS—was overwhelmingly opposed to any further production at the Savannah River Site in general, and the MOX program in particular.

But opposition to SRS projects is largely tempered by support in Aiken and Augusta, two South Carolina cities near the site. Aiken and Augusta derive jobs and economic opportunity from SRS. The area's leading newspaper, "The Augusta Chronicle," for the most part covers SRS activity with bullish enthusiasm.

Ironically, SRS will receive much of its MOX-ready plutonium from Colorado's Rocky Flats, a weapons production facility that has been effectively closed down by unfavorable public opinion. Colorado didn't want that plutonium in its backyard, so the surplus bomb fuel is headed for the southeast which has become the path of least resistance for today's nuclear production.

A Further Health and Safety Risk?

Nuclear Control Institute President Edwin Lyman worries that using MOX fuel in nuclear reactors poses a danger that goes beyond the ordinary risks of nuclear energy.

"The additional public health and environmental risks posed by the substitution of MOX fuel for uranium fuel in light-water reactors have been well-documented, but have not been adequately considered in the DOE NEPA documentation to date," he writes in a memo to NRC. "Furthermore, new information has recently come to light that suggests that the additional risks posed by MOX fuel compared to uranium fuel are even greater than previously assumed."

> *Bringing the plutonium to South Carolina to make MOX was just a guise to get it here to do what the DOE really wants . . . to make new nuclear bombs.*

Savannah residents are concerned about possible health risks associated with MOX production at the Savannah River Site. State Representatives Lester Jackson and Regina Thomas both voiced concern about health impacts at the scoping meeting. Jackson said the Savannah area has a higher rate of cancer and asked what kind of study was being done to measure the possible relationship between that statistic and SRS activity.

Ernie Chapman, from Aiken, cited a state-funded study that shows counties immediately facing the SRS have lower cancer rates than the state average. But neither Jackson nor Thomas seemed convinced that there's no added risk to the Savannah area.

Thomas said she was "very disappointed that costs are more important than human lives."

Jackson also asked whether there might be a link between SRS activity and Savannah's high infant mortality rate to which there was no specific response.

"Cancer isn't necessarily the best indicator of a problem," says Barczak who thinks the infant mortality question needs further study. "We tend not to study those registries. We don't have the infrastructure there where we're doing that nationally," she says.

A Welfare Program for the Nuclear Industry?

"Immobilization of plutonium is demonstrably cheaper, faster, safer, more secure and less of an environmental threat than the MOX approach," writes Lyman. "The sole obstacle to implementation of this clearly superior technology is the political opposition of entrenched nuclear bureaucrats in both the U.S. and Russia, who favor reactor options on ideological grounds, no matter what the cost and risk."

Lyman is but one MOX opponent who questions whether DOE sincerely consulted the public's best interests in opting for MOX production instead of immobilization. Because federal funds will be used to build the new MOX facility, many environmentalists describe the MOX program as a federal subsidy of the nuclear industry.

At the recent scoping meeting in Savannah, Green Party leader William Pleasant described the MOX proposal as "a welfare program for Duke Power" which owns the nuclear stations where MOX will be shipped and used. Lanier, too, described the project as "a big waste of tax dollars."

Other MOX opponents, including Fred Nadelman and Judy Jennings, a local Sierra Club leader, indicated that the MOX program constitutes a handout to the nuclear power business.

The DOE's proposal to burn MOX at only two reactor sites looks modest in comparison to the number of reactors using MOX in Europe. But will that be the end of MOX production in the US, or will the MOX program branch out and serve other nuclear stations?

Lyman writes that much more MOX has been scheduled

for production than can be burned at the McGuire and Catawba nuclear stations slated to receive it.

"NRC should realize that at least three additional reactors will be required to dispose of 3.5 MT of plutonium per year . . . rather than the two reactors that DOE has said would be sufficient," Lyman writes. "NRC must also consider the distinct possibility that DOE will not be able to locate any additional reactors willing to accept the costs and risks of MOX use."

But nowhere in its recently published fact sheets do Duke COGEMA Stone and Webster promise that MOX use will stay confined to those two stations.

To muddy matters some more, the DOE recently announced that the Savannah River Site is in the running for yet another project, this one a "modern pit facility," which Barczak interprets to mean "a site that could produce/manufacture new plutonium pits for nuclear bombs."

"Many have felt all along that bringing the plutonium to South Carolina to make MOX was just a guise to get it here to do what the DOE really wants . . . to make new nuclear bombs," she says.

12

Electronic Waste Is a Serious Problem

Keirsten Scanlon

Keirsten Scanlon works as a business consultant, developing and implementing marketing plans and sales training programs. She is also an undergraduate business instructor at California State University, Sacramento.

With millions of Americans annually replacing obsolete computers, cell phones, and other electronic equipment, the United States is facing an unparalleled toxic waste crisis. Discarded electronics—or e-waste—is loaded with materials such as lead, dioxins, cadmium, and mercury that are hazardous to human health and the environment. When e-waste is thrown into landfills the contaminants leach into local drinking water. When it is burned, harmful pollution is released into the air. The electronics industry has done little to alleviate this problem and the costs of e-waste disposal is largely being shouldered by local governments that are already overburdened by underfunded household hazardous waste programs. The U.S. government needs to require that electronics manufacturers take personal responsibility for the recovery and recycling of e-waste.

E lectronic waste (E-waste) encompasses a broad and growing range of electronic devices ranging from large household appliances such as refrigerators, washers and dryers, and air conditioners, to hand-held cellular phones, fluorescent lamp bulbs (tubes), and personal stereos. Where once consumers purchased a stereo console or television set with the expecta-

Keirsten Scanlon, "Poison PCs and Toxic TVs," www.svtc.org, June 19, 2001, pp. 1–5, 27. Copyright © 2001 by the Silicon Valley Toxics Coalition. Reproduced by permission.

tion that it would last for a decade or more, the increasingly rapid evolution of technology has effectively rendered everything "disposable." Consumers no longer take a malfunctioning toaster, VCR or telephone to a repair shop. Replacement is often easier and cheaper than repair. And while these ever improving gadgets—faster, smaller, cheaper—provide many benefits, they also carry a legacy of waste.

> *Studies estimate that the number of obsolete computers in the United States will soon be as high as 315 to 680 million units.*

Electronic waste already constitutes from 2% to 5% of the US municipal solid waste stream and is growing rapidly. European studies estimate that the volume of electronic waste is rising by 3% to 5% per year—almost three times faster than the municipal waste stream.

According to the US Environmental Protection Agency (EPA), in 1997 more than 3.2 million tons of E-waste ended up in US landfills. In a [2003] report for the EPA, analysts estimate that the amount of E-waste in US landfills will grow fourfold in the next few years.

Over the last several years, no product so epitomizes the problems posed by obsolete electronics as the personal computer. Due to their growing waste volume, toxicity and management cost, they are the focus of this report. How California chooses to address the problems posed by obsolete computers is likely to set the tone for the broader spectrum of E-waste.

A Serious Problem

Today's computer industry innovates very rapidly, bringing new technologies and "upgrades" to market on the average of every 18 months. The average life span of a personal computer has shrunk from four or five years to two years. Users in California buy more than 2.2 million new computer systems each year. Currently, about 50% of US households own a computer.

Analysts estimate that more than 6,000 computers become obsolete in California every day. They are either tossed out with the trash and subsequently landfilled by trash collectors—often illegally—or stored in attics and garages for a later day when they will be dumped.

Consumers have, on average, 2 to 3 obsolete computers in their garages, closets or storage spaces. US government researchers estimate that three-quarters of all computers ever sold in the United States remain stockpiled, awaiting disposal. Should every consumer attempt to throw out their obsolete computer at once, California and the nation would face a major budgetary and environmental crisis.

The crisis continues to grow. Studies estimate that the number of obsolete computers in the United States will soon be as high as 315 to 680 million units. By the year 2005, one computer will become obsolete for every new computer put on the market.

Low Recycling Rates for Computers

The National Safety Council reported in 1999 that only 11% of discarded computers were recycled, compared with 28% of overall municipal solid waste. In California, estimates of computer recycling range from 5% to 15%, compared to a 42% rate for overall solid waste and a 70% rate for major appliances like refrigerators, washing machines, and dryers.

For large commercial customers, computer system distributors may negotiate for the collection and management of obsolete computer systems. However, there remains very little information on where and if these computers are recycled.

For the individual consumer looking to properly manage an obsolete home or office computer, options for recycling are virtually nonexistent. Recycling options that do exist typically come with a price tag of $10 to $30 per unit.

Discarded Computers Are Hazardous Waste

The cathode ray tubes (CRTs) in computer monitors, television sets, and other video display devices contain significant concentrations of lead and other heavy metals. [In 2001] the State of California . . . affirmed that: ". . . when discarded, CRTs are identified as hazardous waste under both federal and State law and are required to be managed in accordance with all applicable requirements, including generator, transporter and facility requirements."

As a hazardous waste, the disposal of CRTs in municipal solid waste landfills is prohibited. Additionally, collection, whether for recycling or disposal, must be regulated and permitted as a hazardous waste activity.

Each computer or television display contains an average of 4 to 8 pounds of lead. The 315 million computers that will become obsolete between 1997 and 2004 contain a total of more than 1.2 billion pounds of lead. Monitor glass contains about 20% lead by weight. When these components are illegally disposed and crushed in landfills, the lead is released into the environment, posing a hazardous legacy for current and future generations. Consumer electronics already constitute 40% of lead found in landfills. About 70% of the heavy metals (including mercury and cadmium) found in landfills comes from electronic equipment discards. These heavy metals and other hazardous substances found in electronics can contaminate groundwater and pose other environmental and public health risks.

> *The 315 million computers that will become obsolete . . . contain a total of more than 1.2 billion pounds of lead.*

Lead can cause damage to the central and peripheral nervous systems, blood system and kidneys in humans. Lead accumulates in the environment, and has highly acute and chronic toxic effects on plants, animals and microorganisms. Children suffer developmental effects and loss of mental ability, even at low levels of exposure.

Other hazardous materials used in computers and other electronic devices include cadmium, mercury, hexavalent chromium, PVC plastic and brominated flame retardants. Mercury, for example, leaches when certain electronic devices such as circuit breakers are destroyed. The presence of halogenated hydrocarbons in computer plastics may result in the formation of dioxin if the plastic is burned. The presence of these chemicals also makes computer recycling particularly hazardous to workers, as well as the environment.

What Should We Do with Obsolete Computers?

Recycling of computer materials and components—when properly implemented—represents the safest and most cost effective strategy for addressing the problems posed by inoperative or outdated computers. Recycling computer materials and components and removing and/or reducing and treating the hazardous components conserves resources, reduces environmental and public health threats, and protects worker safety, while substantially reducing the high cost of permanently storing and disposing of hazardous wastes in permitted hazardous waste facilities.

Computers, televisions and other e-scrap contain valuable materials and components that are technically recyclable. The problem is the lack of collection incentives and recycling infrastructure, as well as the high cost of material collection, handling and processing.

Estimates for the cost of recycling computers range from $10 to $30 per unit. While this is less expensive than the estimated $25 to $50 per unit cost for disposal, someone must still pay these costs.

Even if recycling levels were to double, the total cost of managing California's current output of obsolete computer scrap will range from $25 million to $42 million annually. Add to that the cost of cleaning up the last two decades' legacy of stockpiled obsolete computers, and the total cost over the next 5 years could easily range from $500 million to over $1 billion.

If the task is left to local governments, the management of obsolete computer monitors alone is likely to double both the volume and cost of already overburdened and under-funded household hazardous waste (HHW) programs.

> *Estimates for the cost of recycling computers range from $10 to $30 per unit.*

Consumers and local governments have neither the technical ability nor financial resources to address this problem on their own.

Recently, some local governments and at least two computer manufacturers have established "pay-as-you-go" collection programs that require consumers and small businesses to pay a fee in order to drop off or ship their obsolete computers for recycling. Costs for these programs range from $7 to $30 or more per unit. These programs are doomed to failure.

It is appropriate to internalize the cost of proper waste management into the price of electronic devices at the time of purchase. However, requiring consumers and small business generators to pay the cost of recycling and/or disposal on the back end has proven to be a shortsighted and ultimately ineffective approach. As we have seen firsthand in California, reliance on back end disposal fees—such as those currently in place for used tires—reduces incentives for proper recycling, encourages 'sham' recycling, and results in improper and often illegal disposal which ultimately requires cleanup at a substantial cost to taxpayers.

IBM sold more than 3 million computers in the United States last year [2000] and was the first manufacturer to establish a pay-as-you-go system for recycling obsolete computers. So far, the results have been underwhelming. According to the company, less than 1,000 computers (0.03% of annual sales) have been recycled under this system. . . .

Europe has taken the lead in addressing the E-waste problem by proposing an ambitious system of "extended producer responsibility." In May of 2001, the European Union (EU) Parliament adopted a directive that requires producers of electronics to take responsibility—financial and otherwise—for the recovery and recycling of E-waste. A second directive requires manufacturers to phase out the use of hazardous materials. California should follow the EU's lead.

13

Cars and Roads
Are a Major Source
of Toxic Waste

Richard T.T. Forman et al.

Richard T.T. Forman is a professor of landscape ecology at Harvard University Graduate School of Design.

While hazardous waste disposal areas are often isolated far away from communities, a major source of toxic waste is as close as the nearest highway. With hundreds of millions of cars traveling America's roads every day, roads are repositories of petrochemical waste, poisonous fluids, and toxic particles that wear off of tires, brakes, and other vehicle parts. In addition, some roads themselves are built with harmful substances such as contaminated soil and demolition waste. Unlike many other hazardous waste sources, toxins generated by automobiles are rarely quantified or studied. When people walk, bike, or play near the side of a road, they seldom think that they are occupying a hazardous waste site. However, because of the pollution generated by cars and trucks, roadbeds are dangerous to human health and the environment.

A rich assortment of invisible chemicals accumulates along roads. The mixture is served up by vehicles, roadside management, and the roads themselves. In low amounts, the substances are just as benign as the chemical array served up by nature. But in high amounts—that is, levels unwanted by society

—the added chemicals become pollutants or contaminants.

Some chemicals accumulating along roads are transported short distances through the air, but most are carried by water washing off (or seeping through) a road. . . .

The effect of roads on water quality is a concern to water resource managers, highway departments, and many other people concerned with environmental conditions. . . . The chemicals added along roads affect far more than water. They build up in the soil, in plants, and in animals, with consequent cascading effects through terrestrial ecosystems.

Sources of Chemical Pollutants

Chemical substances, of course, are everywhere on earth, but polluting levels of chemicals cause damage or toxic reactions to human health, to ecological systems, or to both. Here we focus on the chemicals that inhibit natural processes and native species. Major sources of roadside pollutants are vehicles, roads and bridges, and dry and wet (dust and rain) atmospheric deposition. Localized, less-frequent sources include spills of oil, gasoline (petrol), industrial chemicals, and other substances, and losses of materials in accidents involving vehicles and roadside structures. In addition, objects discarded from vehicles accumulate along many roads. Roadway maintenance practices, such as sanding and de-icing road surfaces and applying herbicides to roadsides, usually add pollutants. Also, both the road surface and the tires rolling on it gradually degrade.

> *One assessment of chemicals found along roads indicates that 19 of the 23 important pollutants (83%) come from vehicles.*

One assessment of chemicals found along roads indicates that 19 of the 23 important pollutants (83%) come from vehicles. Within vehicles, there are several major sources of pollutants, and a particular type of pollutant can come from a number of sources. Thus one-third (35%) of the types of roadside pollutants come from oil, grease, and hydraulic fluids. Engine and parts wear produces 30% of the pollutant types; metal plating and rust, 22%; tire wear, 22%; fuel and exhaust, 22%; and brake lining wear, 17%. Similarly, nonvehicular sources pro-duce many types of pollutants. Sanding and de-icing agents produce one-fifth (22%) of the pollutant types; roadbed and road surface wear, 17%; and herbicide and pesticide use, 13%. These figures do not include heavy metals and other chemicals that leach from bridges into streams and other water bodies. In short, chemical pollutants along roads originate from diverse sources, and even significantly reducing a single pollutant would normally require control of a number of the sources.

Roads, Roadsides, and Management

Since road networks slice through or surround most ecosystems, and because road surfaces degrade between resurfacings, the composition of road surfaces is of ecological interest. Two bil-lion metric tons of total solid waste are produced annually in the USA. Eighty percent is mineral waste from mining, 10% is municipal solid waste, and 5% (about 100,000 tons) is asphalt road-surface material annually removed from roads. To reduce the amount of waste for disposal and the amount of new as-phalt containing petroleum products, 80% of the road-surface material removed is recycled back into new road surfaces. Al-though few data are readily available on amounts and fre-quency, in some cases road recycling or resurfacing projects in-clude recycled asphalt pavement, blast furnace slag, coal fly ash, cement kiln dust, or steel slag. Apparently, smaller amounts of nonferrous slags, reclaimed concrete, coal bottom ash, and boiler ash may also be included in recycled road material. In various European countries, many other materials are compo-nents of recycled road material, including municipal solid waste, coal mining waste, dredged material (e.g., from harbors), gypsum, phosphorus slag, slightly contaminated soil (and heav-ily contaminated soil after cleaning), demolition waste, coal fly ash (silico-aluminius), tires, and plastics.

Road surface degradation over several years leads to surface distress, deformation, or cracks. This may permit rainwater or snowmelt to penetrate into the surface and base of a road, leaching chemicals that reach surrounding ecosystems. Resur-facing follows, increasingly using recycled materials in the USA. Water and wind sweep across road surfaces carrying road particles into nearby or downwind ecosystems. Eroded road particles are also lifted into the air by the turbulence of passing vehicles. Unfortunately, little information is available on the chemical composition of different roads or whether these inputs are important ecologically in ecosystems.

Finally, in road construction, fill material trucked in to construct a road (or topsoil used on the roadside) may be chemically quite distinct from that of the roadside or adjacent area. Limestone-derived fill material placed over an acidic granite-derived substrate, or vice versa, illustrates this point. In this case, chemicals from the roadbed would change the soil pH and plants of an adjacent zone. Aquatic ecosystems in streams alongside of or downstream from such a roadbed would have an altered water quality.

Vehicles, Tires, and Fuel

Several types of chemical pollutants originate from vehicles. Gradual or chronic wear, leaks, and emissions from exhaust of moving vehicles tend to widely distribute the chemicals along a road, where they accumulate.

Vehicles leak or spill several polluting materials:

• *Mineral nutrients.* Road runoff may include nitrogen or phosphorus, which can be nutrient-polluting (eutrophication) sources in aquatic ecosystems.

• *Heavy metals.* Runoff may include metals such as zinc and cadmium from vehicle wear, combustion products, catalytic converters, abrasives in brake linings, and uncombusted fuel additives.

• *Organic compounds.* Most organic compounds found in runoff are from exhaust (uncombusted products), spilled fuels, lubricants, coolants, and hydraulic fluids. Petroleum products are mainly composed of diverse *hydrocarbons*, which primarily consist of carbon and hydrogen. *Polycyclic aromatic hydrocarbons* are usually formed in incomplete combustion and are generally volatile, but they also can be found in runoff sediments. *Mono-aromatic hydrocarbon compounds* are common in crude oil and petroleum products, and find their way into runoff primarily through spills and leaks of gasoline and other petroleum products.

One increasing concern regarding hydrocarbons is the impact of ultraviolet (UV) radiation. The toxicity of hydrocarbons to aquatic organisms seems to be greatly increased by UV radiation from sunlight.

A series of chemical additives to gasoline used to increase combustion efficiency has been a particular pollution problem.

Tetraethyl lead was introduced as an antiknock compound for gasoline engines in 1922. The resulting lead pollution (and consequent problems with newly introduced catalytic converters on vehicles) caused the USA to shift to unleaded gasoline in 1974. Canada and Europe switched to unleaded fuels 15 to 20 years later. Although some of the lead from fuel remains in the roadside environment, particularly somewhat deeper in the soil profile, lead levels in plants and animals overall have dropped significantly since lead was removed from fuel.

As a substitute for lead, manganese-containing fuel additives were used extensively in the mid-1970s and early 1980s but supposedly were discontinued soon thereafter, *MMT* (methyl cyclopentadienyl manganese tricarbonyl) then replaced tetraethyl lead as the antiknock compound in some gasolines. The combustion of fuels with MMT produces vehicle exhaust containing manganese oxides.

> *Resurfacing projects include recycled asphalt pavement, blast furnace slag, coal fly ash, cement kiln dust, or steel slag.*

Although manganese oxides can clearly cause negative health effects in animals and humans in laboratory studies, the amount of manganese added to the environment from exhaust is not currently considered a significant ecological risk. Nonetheless, a consensus exists calling for a better understanding of human-caused manganese oxides in the environment and their potential effects on humans and nature. One recent study in Utah reported soil manganese concentrations along interstate freeways with high traffic volume (70,000–148,000 [vehicles per day]) up to 100 times higher than historic levels. The investigators also found that roadside aquatic plants were higher in leaf-tissue manganese than were herbs or grasses, and that submerged and emergent aquatic plants were particularly sensitive bio-indicators of manganese contamination.

One of the most ubiquitous indirect examples of motor vehicle–associated pollution in recent years has been the spread of *MTBE* (methyl tertiary-butyl ether), which in a study of 16 cities was found in 7% of the stormwater drains. MTBE improves the combustion of gasoline and is an additive to reduce ozone emissions in some regions. Although MTBE is volatile in the air, the primary pollution concern is the presence of leaking fuel tanks among the thousands of gas stations that use underground storage (regulations require testing and replacement of tanks as appropriate). Most of the hydrocarbons that compose gasoline move relatively slowly through soil, which means that they accumulate and may be amenable to site-specific cleanup. In contrast, MTBE is highly soluble, spreads rapidly through groundwater, and persists a long time. That poses a different and more serious problem. The MTBE additive readily reaches and contaminates aquifers as well as streams and lakes.

Areas adjacent to major highways receive the greatest input of heavy metal particles. On both sides of such highways, a distinct gradient of elevated concentration typically extends outward for up to about 50 to 100 m (165 to 330 ft). Increased concentrations have been found in air, soil, and plants within this zone. Toxic levels of heavy metals may extend outward for meters rather than tens of meters, though this certainly varies by species. It is important to know how these contaminants are distributed and their potential effects, because they may adversely affect all forms of life in an area, including humans.

> *More than a half million shipments of hazardous materials are carried daily on the U.S. road network.*

Rubber from tires also accumulates along roads. Highway travel usually means passing "road-kill mimics," the black chunks of shredded truck tires that at first glance resemble creature forms, from dead dogs to squashed snakes. Unnoticed and more important environmentally are the fine particles of rubber and its various synthetic forms that result from incessant tire wear along the road. Roughly one tire per year per car on average is discarded after distributing its tread in particles along the road network. For example, in the former West Germany, which has a much smaller area but a highway density more than twice that of the USA, it is estimated that 1 mm of road surface material is annually eroded from the highways (1 in 25 years). On the same road system, 100,000 tons of tire dust are annually generated. Wind and the turbulence of passing vehicles raise the tire dust and other particles into the air to be deposited downwind. Furthermore, rain and snowmelt periodically wash the particles into aquatic environments.

Chemical Spills

The road network is a thoroughfare for passenger vehicles and for trucks carrying freight, some of it toxic chemical substances. More than a half million shipments of hazardous materials are carried daily on the U.S. road network. A small fraction is spilled, though this includes some large spills and some next to water supplies and sensitive ecosystems.

In the USA, about 2,400 accidental chemical spills are reported each year to the federal government. The actual number of spills, plus the illegal dumping of chemicals (and washing of chemical-carrying trucks) while standing or moving along roads, is unknown. In addition, 7 million vehicle accidents, most of which release some chemical pollution onto the road, are annually distributed over 6.2 million km (3.9 million mi) of public roads. This combined process distributes the gasoline, oil, and other leakage pollutants through much of the road network. Roadsides, groundwater, and nearby aquatic ecosystems are major recipients of the concentrated pollutant mixture. Most roads are bordered by ditches that carry water rapidly and directly to streams, lakes, and other water bodies. Therefore, chemical spills that pollute aquatic environments are probably a fairly common occurrence, though the frequency, amounts, and ecological effects are unknown.

> *Temporary and accidental pollution sources . . . can be toxic to different organisms and can degrade local ecosystems.*

An overview of the transportation-related pollutants and their primary sources emphasizes that no "magic answer" will be found as a solution. Most pollutants come from multiple sources, which can be *temporary* (pollution due to road construction or maintenance), *chronic* (vehicle exhaust, pavement and tire wear), *seasonal* (de-icing in winter), or *accidental* (spillage). The most persistent and problematic sources are chronic and seasonal. Temporary and accidental pollution sources tend to be localized but can be highly concentrated. All can be toxic to different organisms and can degrade local ecosystems.

In view of the array of chemical pollutants originating from roads and vehicles, a set of best management practices has evolved to reduce environmental impacts, especially near sensitive ecosystems and drinking water supplies.

Organizations to Contact

The editors have compiled the following list of organizations concerned with the issues debated in this book. The descriptions are derived from materials provided by the organizations. All have publications or information available for interested readers. The list was compiled on the date of publication of the present volume; the information provided here may change. Be aware that many organizations take several weeks or longer to respond to inquiries, so allow as much time as possible.

American Council on Science and Health (ACSH)
1995 Broadway, 2nd Fl., New York, NY 10023-5860
(212) 362-7044 • fax: (212) 362-4919
e-mail: acsh@acsh.org • Web site: www.acsh.org

The American Council on Science and Health is a consumer education consortium funded by corporations that produce chemicals, oil, alcoholic beverages, fast food, automobiles, and other consumer products. The organization is concerned with issues related to food, nutrition, chemicals, pharmaceuticals, the environment, and health.

Carnegie Endowment for International Peace
1779 Massachusetts Ave. NW, Washington, DC 20036
(202) 483-7600 • fax: (202) 483-1840
e-mail: info@ceip.org • Web site: www.ceip.org

The Carnegie Endowment for International Peace conducts research on international affairs and U.S. foreign policy. Issues concerning nuclear weapons and proliferation are often discussed in articles published in its quarterly journal *Foreign Policy*.

Center for Defense Information (CDI)
1779 Massachusetts Ave. NW, Suite 615, Washington, DC 20036
(202) 332-0600 • fax: (202) 462-4559
e-mail: info@cdi.org • Web site: www.cdi.org

CDI comprises civilians and former military officers who oppose both policies that increase the danger of war and excessive expenditures for weapons. The center serves as an independent monitor of the military, analyzing spending, policies, weapon systems, and related military issues. It publishes the *Defense Monitor* ten times per year.

Center for Nonproliferation Studies
Monterey Institute for International Studies
425 Van Buren St., Monterey, CA 93940
(831) 647-4154 • fax: (831) 647-3519
Web site: http://cns.miis.edu

The Center for Nonproliferation Studies researches all aspects of nonproliferation, works to combat the spread of weapons of mass destruction, and proposes measures to avert nuclear terrorism. The center produces research databases and has multiple reports, papers, speeches, and congressional testimony available online. Its main publication is the *Nonproliferation Review*, which is published three times per year.

Chemical Weapons Working Group (CWWG)
PO Box 467, Berea, KY 40403
(859) 986-7565 • fax: (859) 986-2695
e-mail: kefcwwg@acs.eku.edu • Web site: www.cwwg.org

The Chemical Weapons Working Group is an international coalition of citizens living near chemical weapons storage sites in the United States, the Pacific, and Russia, and who will be most affected by the disposal of these munitions. The CWWG's mission is to oppose incineration of chemical weapons as an unsafe disposal method and to work with all appropriate political bodies to ensure the safe disposal of these munitions and other chemical warfare and toxic material. The group publishes a newsletter, *Common Sense*, and its Web site offers various reports concerning chemical weapons storage and disposal issues.

Competitive Enterprise Institute (CEI)
1001 Connecticut Ave. NW, Suite 1250, Washington, DC 20036
(202) 331-1010 • fax: (202) 331-0640
e-mail: info@cei.org • Web site: www.cei.org

The Competitive Enterprise Institute encourages the use of the free market and private property rights to protect the environment. It advocates removing governmental regulatory barriers and establishing a system in which the private sector would be responsible for the environment. CEI's publications include the monthly newsletter *CEI Update* and editorials in its *On Point* series.

Henry L. Stimson Center
11 Dupont Circle NW, 9th Fl., Washington, DC 20036
(202) 223-5956 • fax: (202) 238-9604
Web site: www.stimson.org

The Stimson Center is an independent nonprofit public policy institute committed to finding and promoting innovative solutions to the security challenges confronting the United States and other nations. The center directs the Chemical and Biological Weapons Nonproliferation Project, which serves as a clearinghouse of information related to the monitoring and implementation of the 1993 Chemical Weapons Convention. The center produces occasional papers, reports, handbooks, and books on chemical and biological weapon policy, nuclear policy, and eliminating weapons of mass destruction.

Institute for Energy and Environmental Research (IEER)
6935 Laurel Ave., Suite 204, Takoma Park, MD 20912
(301) 270-5500
e-mail: ieer@ieer.org • Web site: www.ieer.org/ieerinfo.html

The Institute for Energy and Environmental Research was organized to provide scientifically researched information to people who are not scientists. Activists concerned about the environment and other progressive issues can purchase dozens of books and access technical reports and fact sheets on the group's Web site. The IEER also publishes two newsletters, *Science for Democratic Action* and *Energy and Security*.

Military Toxics Project
PO Box 558, Lewiston, ME 04243
(207) 783-5091
e-mail: tara@miltoxproj.org • Web site: www.miltoxproj.org

The mission of the Military Toxics Project is to unite activists, organizations, and communities in the struggle to clean up military pollution, safeguard the transportation of hazardous materials, and to advance the development and implementation of preventative solutions to the toxic and radioactive pollution caused by military activities.

Nuclear Information and Resource Service and World Information Service on Energy (NIRS/WISE)
1424 Sixteenth St. NW, Suite 404, Washington, DC 20036
(202) 328-0002 • fax: (202) 462-2183
e-mail: nirsnet@nirs.org • Web site: www.nirs.org

The Nuclear Information and Resource Service and World Information Service on Energy is an information and networking center for citizens and environmental organizations concerned about nuclear power, radioactive waste, radiation, and sustainable energy issues.

Public Citizen
215 Pennsylvania Ave. SE, Washington, DC 20003
(202) 546-4996 • fax: (202) 547-7392
e-mail: cmep@citizen.org • Web site: www.citizen.org/cmep

Public Citizen is a national nonprofit consumer advocacy organization founded in 1971 to represent consumer interests in Congress, the executive branch, and the courts. Public Citizen fights for openness and democratic accountability in government; for the right of consumers to seek redress in the courts; for clean, safe, and sustainable energy sources; for social and economic justice in trade policies; for strong health, safety, and environmental protections; and for safe, effective, and affordable prescription drugs and health care.

Silicon Valley Toxics Coalition (SVTC)
760 N. First St., San Jose, CA 95112
(408) 287-6707 • fax: (408) 287-6771
e-mail: svtc@svtc.org • Web site: www.svtc.org

Silicon Valley Toxics Coalition is a grassroots coalition concerned with the environmental and human health problems caused by the rapid growth of the high-tech electronics industry. The coalition engages in research and advocacy regarding issues such as environmental sustainability, clean production of computers, and democratic decision making for communities and workers.

U.S. Department of Energy
1000 Independence Ave. SW, Washington, DC 20585
(800) DIAL-DOE • fax: (202) 586-8800
Web site: www.energy.gov/engine/content.do

The Department of Energy's overarching mission is to advance the national, economic, and energy security of the United States; to promote scientific and technological innovation in support of that mission; and to ensure the environmental cleanup of the national nuclear weapons complex.

U.S. PIRG
218 D St. SE, Washington, DC 20003
(202) 546-9707 • fax: (202) 546-2461
e-mail: uspirg@uspirg.org • Web site: www.uspirg.org

PIRGs are Public Interest Research Groups that are active in all fifty states as watchdogs for the public interest. The state PIRGs created U.S. Public Interest Research Group (U.S. PIRG) in 1983 to perform the same functions in the nation's capital. U.S. PIRG advocates grassroots viewpoints and attempts to influence the national policy debate in order to protect the environment; encourage a fair, sustainable economy; and foster responsive, democratic government.

Bibliography

Books

Len Ackland	*Making a Real Killing: Rocky Flats and the Nuclear West.* Albuquerque: University of New Mexico Press, 2002.
Donald L. Barlett and James B. Steele	*Forevermore: Nuclear Waste in America.* New York: W.W. Norton, 1986.
Tad Bartimus and Scott McCartney	*Trinity's Children: Living Along America's Nuclear Highway.* New York: Harcourt Brace Jovanovich, 1991.
Thomas D. Beamish	*Silent Spill: The Organization of an Industrial Crisis.* Cambridge, MA: MIT Press, 2002.
Devra Lee Davis	*When Smoke Ran Like Water: Tales of Environmental Deception and the Battle Against Pollution.* New York: Basic Books, 2002.
Jim Day	*Screw Nevada! A Cartoon Chronicle of the Yucca Mountain Nuke Dump Controversy.* Las Vegas: Stephens, 2002.
William Eggleston	*Los Alamos.* New York: Scalo, 2003.
Kai T. Erickson	*A New Species of Trouble.* New York: W.W. Norton, 1994.
Richard T.T. Forman et al.	*Road Ecology.* Washington, DC: Island, 2003.
Lois Marie Gibbs	*Love Canal: The Story Continues.* San Francisco: New Society, 1998.
Eddie J. Girdner and Jack Smith	*Killing Me Softly: Toxic Waste, Corporate Profit, and the Struggle for Environmental Justice.* New York: Monthly Review, 2002.
Thomas Groeneveld	*Navigating the Waters: Coordination of Waterfront Brownfields Redevelopment.* Washington, DC: ICMA, 2002.
John Harte et al.	*Toxics A to Z: A Guide to Everyday Pollution Hazards.* Berkeley: University of California Press, 1991.
Richard Hofrichter	*Reclaiming the Environmental Debate: The Politics of Health in a Toxic Culture.* Cambridge, MA: MIT Press, 2000.

Richard Hofrichter and   *Toxic Struggles: The Theory and Practice of Environ-*
Michel Gelobter, eds.   *mental Justice.* Salt Lake City: University of Utah
Press, 2002.

Valerie Kuletz   *The Tainted Desert: Environmental and Social Ruin in the American West.* New York: Dimensions, 1998.

Gerald Markowitz   *Deceit and Denial: The Deadly Politics of Industrial*
and David Rosner   *Pollution.* Berkeley: University of California Press, 2003.

Dan McGovern   *The Campo Indian Landfill War: The Fight for Gold in California's Garbage.* Norman: University of Oklahoma Press, 1995.

Katherine N. Probst   *Footing the Bill for the Superfund Cleanups: Who*
et al.   *Pays and How?* Washington, DC: Brookings Institution Press, 1994.

Dianne Rahm, ed.   *Toxic Waste and Environmental Policy in the 21st Century United States.* Jefferson, NC: McFarland, 2002.

Piero Risoluti   *Nuclear Waste: A Technological and Political Challenge.* New York: Springer-Verlag, 2004.

Andrew Schneider   *An Air That Kills: How the Asbestos Poisoning of*
and David McCumber   *Libby, Montana, Uncovered a National Scandal.* New York: G.P. Putnam's Sons, 2004.

Molly Singer   *Small Spaces, Special Places: Coordination of Rural Brownfields Redevelopment.* Washington, DC: ICMA, 2002.

Rebecca Solnit   *Salvage Dreams.* Berkeley: University of California Press, 1999.

Christian Warren   *Brush with Death: A Social History of Lead Poisoning.* Baltimore: Johns Hopkins University Press, 2001.

Periodicals

Jeff Bailey   "Waste of a Sort: Curbside Recycling Comforts the Soul, but Benefits Are Scant," *Wall Street Journal,* January 19, 1995.

Edward Belden   "E-Waste," University of California at Santa Barbara Department of Economics, 2001. www.econ. ucsb.edu/~mcauslan/ESM246/EWaste.pdf.

Chris Bryant   "The Hidden Life of Batteries," *Sierra Magazine,* November/December 2003.

Michael Carrigan   "Accidents Will Happen: Yucca Site Could Direct Radioactive Waste Through Eugene Area," *Eugene Weekly,* June 6, 2002.

Earth 911   "Frequently Asked Questions About Electronics and the Environment," July 30, 2003. www. earth911.org.

Bob Fernandez "Rules Let Contaminants Be Covered, Not Cleaned," *Philadelphia Inquirer*, April 13, 1999.

Jim Hightower "Stop the Stupidity at Yucca Mountain," *San Antonio Current*, March 6, 2002.

Lindsey Hodel "Cell-Ing Out," *Mother Earth News*, October/November 2003.

Tara Hulen "Dispatch from Toxic Town: Ten Years Ago, a Fisherman Pulled a Bass Out of the Choccolocco. For the People of Anniston, Alabama, Life Hasn't Been the Same Since," *OnEarth*, Winter 2003.

Jane Katz "What a Waste: The Generation and Disposal of Trash Imposes Costs on Society and the Environment. Should We Be Doing More?" *Regional Review*, March 2002.

Military Toxics Project "The U.S. Military's Environmental Assault on Communities," Environmental Health Coalition, June 2001. www.miltoxproj.org/magnacarta/DefendOurHealthReport.html.

Paul Mohai "African American Concern for the Environment," *Environment*, June 2003.

Christopher E. Paine "Weaponeers of Waste: A Critical Look at the Bush Administration Energy Department's Nuclear Weapons Complex and the First Decade of Science-Based Stockpile Stewardship," Natural Resources Defense Council, April 2004. www.nrdc.org/nuclear/weaponeers/weaponeers.pdf.

Ed Rampell "The Military's Mess: Johnston Atoll, the Army's 'Model' Chemical Disposal Facility, Is an Environmental Disaster," *E*, January/February 1996.

Jana Richman "A Cloud over My Hometown," *Progressive*, February 2000.

Dan Rosenheck "Digging a Deeper and Deeper Hole: America's Nuclear Waste Storage Project at Yucca Mountain," *New Statesman*, September 29, 2003.

Peter Sampson "Something Foul Is Spreading in the Ground," *Bergen Record*, May 14, 1999.

Ron Schneiderman "Electronic Waste: Be Part of the Solution: Environmentally Conscious Designs, Take-Back Programs, and Legislative Measures Aimed to Embed More Recycling Within the Electronics Culture," *Electronic Design*, April 12, 2004.

Michael Shore et al. "Stop Blowing Smoke in the Heartland," Environmental Defense, August 16, 2004. www.environmentaldefense.org/documents/3887_blowing smoke.pdf.

Shundahai Network   "Yucca Mountain Information," August 2004. www.shundahai.org/yucca_mt.html.

Scott Sonner   "Nuclear Expert: Yucca Unsafe—Scientist Quits Panel So He Could Speak Out," *Las Vegas Sun*, February 19, 2004.

Tina Susman   "Alabama Town Wary as Army Begins Destroying Weapons Stockpile," *Newsday*, August 5, 2003.

Jonathan B. Tucker   "Chemical Weapons: Buried in the Backyard," *Bulletin of the Atomic Scientists*, September 2001.

Leslie Valentine   "Chemical Imbalance: The Gaping Hole in Our Nation's Security," Environmental Defense, September 11, 2002. www.environmentaldefense.org/article.cfm?contentid=2290.

John C. Zink   "For Yucca Mountain, Less Is More," *Power Engineering*, May 2004.

Index